I0171620

Unending Love:
The Gift of Faith

STEVEN M. PAINTER

CRUCSON
PUBLISHING

Library of Congress number: 2016905153

Cover Design: Daniel B. Gonzales (www.danielbgonzales.com)

For more information check out:

www.stevenmpainter.com

ISBN: 978-0-9889743-2-6

10 9 8 7 6 5 4 3 2 1

TO TED AND ERIC,

For helping me on the path to Christ.

CONTENTS

INTRODUCTION

My purpose in writing this book is to reach the fence-sitters. These are the people who go to church on Christmas and Easter. Perhaps they believe that Jesus of Nazareth was a great moral teacher. They may even believe there is a supreme being called God. But they are not willing to fully commit to becoming Christian.

Attending church every week can be too much of a hassle. Priests have been involved in scandals throughout the history of Christianity. In fact, much blood has been shed in the name of Christ and God. This can be disconcerting to someone who wishes to believe in the goodness of God and knows that there is something more in the world besides human beings, animals, and that elusive entity we call nature. Why believe in the goodness of God and the church when those who are supposed to be Christian leaders do not follow the teachings of Jesus?

There is also the resistance toward Jesus of Nazareth being Jesus Christ, the Chosen One, the Messiah, the Son of God. How can God have a son? How can God die? How can God die such a brutal death? How could people in the first century not recognize they were killing the Son of God? Why didn't Jesus perform grand miracles or directly announce his being God to the world? How can the death of one man clear the world of sin? What exactly is sin?

The concept of sin can be difficult for someone unfamiliar with Christianity to wrap their head around. There is also the difficulty of believing in an all-seeing and all-knowing God. What exactly does God look like? If He isn't visible then isn't he just an imaginary friend? Is He a face in the clouds? Or is that just a popular image taken from Roman and Greek mythology of gods like Zeus or Jupiter? Does He always appear in non-human form, like the burning bush to Moses? What about the idea that He created human beings in His image? Does that mean He walks, talks, and looks like a human being? How can He be all-seeing and all-knowing then?

The truth is, it is a lot easier not to believe in God. Life is so much simpler if Jesus was just a great moral teacher and the world is governed by ideas like nature, karma, and coincidence. These ideas are not completely abstract. Science helps us discern the laws of nature. We have all experienced something that we believe to be a coincidence. Karma is probably the most abstract of the three ideas mentioned above. There are those who believe a person's actions have the power to influence future events in that person's life, for better or worse. Yet, these same people will go running away from you when you bring up the possibility of God being at work in the world and not karma, nature, or coincidence.

I used to be a fence-sitter with plenty of questions about God. It took time to get my questions answered. It was not an easy process. But at the end of the day, I wouldn't change that process for anything. Believing in God is the best thing that ever happened to me. It's the toughest and most rewarding thing I've ever done in my life. I graduated from high school. I graduated from college. I graduated from graduate school. All those graduation ceremonies and accomplishments meant less to me than my baptism ceremony. I learned more in the process of coming to accept Jesus and God than I ever did in a classroom.

As someone who considers himself to be intelligent, I want to address some of the concerns fence-sitters may have about God. I want to rationally and reasonably explain some of the struggles I went through in accepting God. I hope that my words are able to answer some of your questions and fears about God. I am not a preacher. I do not have a background in religious studies. I am just like you. I'm a common man with a reasonable amount of intelligence – just like you.

You will read about my personal story in believing in God and Jesus Christ in the next chapter. The chapters following my conversion story will deal with some of the questions I had about God. I will address the topics of evolution, sin, the historical Jesus, the Gospels as eye-witness testimony, suffering, and several other topics that I struggle with even now, such as angels, demons, and hell. I provide my reasoning and logic for reaching my conclusions in each chapter. In this way, I am able to use the cornerstones of the atheist religion to strengthen my belief in God. I possess an analytic mind, so reason and logic were the only ways that I could come to the conclusion that God and Jesus Christ were real and necessary to add to my life in order for me to be happy in this world.

Finally, I have included a chapter called "A Prescription for Christians" at the end of this book. It is easy to be caught up in the material world of twenty-first century living. It is difficult to remain grounded in Jesus and God without consistently reading, listening, and living the word of God.

The pages that follow feature how I came to the conclusion to follow

God and how I plan to keep following Him. I wish you the best of luck in your journey to finding and following God. You will not regret getting off the fence and following the path that leads to Heaven.

1 MY TESTIMONY

Becoming a follower of Jesus was a slow process. Sometimes I wished I could have been blinded for three days and then be a believer, just like the apostle Paul. Instead of taking three days, my process took nearly a year.

I grew up attending church on Easter and Christmas Eve. Then I dropped going to church on Easter. In college, I stopped going on Christmas Eve. I thought it was wonderful. I could celebrate the holidays without having to be religious.

Around the same time I stopped going to church, my sister entered college. One of her roommates was a preacher's daughter. My sister started to attend church through the guidance of her roommate. Eventually my sister became a follower of Christ. I made fun of her for going to church and believing in an imaginary person. I thought she was smart. At least she was when I grew up with her. So why did she need to believe in an imaginary person for strength?

I remained far from church after I graduated college and through my mid-twenties. In 2012 I got a job at a reference book publishing company in Tucson, Arizona. It was a small company. There were only three employees – myself, the boss, and the editor (Eric). Eric was around the same age as me, so we shared similar life experiences. We were able to talk sports, work, and life as adults. After about a year of working together, Eric left the company to become a pastor at a local church.

Shortly after he left, he invited me to play on his church's softball team. We played in a league sponsored by the Jewish Community Center. We weren't good, but I had a lot of fun and enjoyed hanging out with the other guys. I got to meet the lead pastor of the church – Ted. He was nice and outgoing and did not push his religion on me. In fact, nobody pushed religion on me. We just played softball.

I wanted to stay in contact with Eric after the softball season, so we decided to catch a few college baseball games together. At one of the games, I asked Eric about his church. I wanted to go up one Sunday and say hello to him and the rest of the guys. I didn't plan on doing more than just occasionally popping in to see how everyone was doing. Eric gave me the information about service times and the church's address. Like most people who do not go to church often, I put off attending by finding any excuse available. I thought the drive was too far. I didn't want to waste my morning doing something I wouldn't like. There are always a hundred excuses for not doing something.

One Sunday I finally worked up enough courage to attend church. I arrived and there was no Eric. He was on vacation that week. I was extremely uncomfortable, but I decided to make it through the service. I sat down and Ted told the story from the Book of Acts about Philip and the Ethiopian treasurer. The Ethiopian treasurer has been in Jerusalem to worship and was taking the road back from Jerusalem to Ethiopia when Jesus' disciple, Philip, came upon him. The treasurer was reading from the Book of Isaiah and wondering what exactly one of the passages meant. Philip was there to explain that the passage was a prediction of the coming of Jesus. Through a discussion about who Jesus was and what he stood for, Philip was able to convert the treasurer. The story ends with Philip baptizing the man. I had never heard that story before. I was so used to the Jesus birth and death stories while at church for Christmas and Easter that I knew nothing else about the New Testament. Not only was it an interesting story, but it felt like Ted was speaking directly to me. I knew just what the Ethiopian treasurer was going through in trying to figure out if Jesus was really who he said he was or if he was just a myth. Luckily for the Ethiopian treasurer, Philip was told by the Holy Spirit to be right there to answer his questions. I had Ted to answer mine.

The sermon and circumstances of my attending church stuck with me throughout the next day. I sent Ted an e-mail to ask him if it was a coincidence that I attended church on a day Eric wasn't there and that his sermon was the only one I'd ever heard where I felt the pastor was speaking directly to me. By the end of the e-mail, I came to the conclusion that it wasn't a coincidence. I asked him for help in finding out more about God.

Ted, Eric, and my sister all helped out by recommending books for me to read. My analytic mind needed to absorb both sides of the God debate. One of the books recommended was C.S. Lewis's *Mere Christianity*. I'd never read anything like it. I didn't know Christianity could be so logical and intelligent. He made a great case for Christ, but I still needed further convincing.

I did some research into the historical Jesus and the writing of the Gospels. It became clear that Jesus of Nazareth really existed and the Gospels had all the hallmarks of being eyewitness accounts. From there it became a matter of if I believed the words Jesus spoke in the Gospels. The moral teachings of Jesus rang true. But it was also true that those words could not be divorced from his words about the Kingdom of Heaven and his own divinity. So I had no choice but to start believing.

Once I became convinced that Jesus was God, then that meant there was a God and I needed to start finding Him. I joined a small group at church and became exposed to Christians who were more mature in their faith. They helped me along by answering my questions and providing further proof that Christians are not dumb people who are duped into believing in an imaginary friend. Quite the contrary. Christians are intelligent. In fact, I was never as intellectually stimulated by school work like I have been when discussing God.

With my doubts answered, I chose to make a full-time commitment to God. On March 16, 2014 I was baptized. Even though becoming a believer in Jesus might have been quicker for Paul, I would not trade the slow process I went through for anything.

Do not be afraid. The journey you are on is one much traveled. The questions you have are natural. There are many resources out there to help you. The rest of this book will provide some answers to your questions.

2 CREATIONISM VS. EVOLUTION

Evolution vs. creationism is probably the most popular debate between atheists and Christians. Evolution is taught to students in public schools. Some Christians wish that creationism, or intelligent design, be either taught in public schools or at least be an option for students. Evolution has become so ingrained in public schools that it was all I learned throughout my scholarly career. I took the usual biology course in high school and then took two anthropology courses in college. I found anthropology to be one of the easiest courses I took, which is why I wanted to take two courses. It was a great deal like history for me. I enjoy history, so I looked at anthropology as just the history of the human race. I accepted the teachings with few questions. The evidence seemed to be overwhelming for evolution. The arguments I heard for creationism weren't too convincing.

The usual argument for creationism involves the Bible. There are literal believers in the Bible who will debate you over how the writings of the Bible are God's words and cannot be questioned. I am not one of those people. The literal believers are holding back the more intriguing arguments that can be made regarding creationism. The Bible can be used as a starting point, but the tools that atheists frequently use to explain nature via observation and reason along with unanswered evolutionary questions provide the main bulk of the argument for creationism.

Chapter 5 on the Gospels as eyewitness accounts will provide the bulk of my argument regarding my unbelief in the literal view of the Bible. For now, let me say that although it can be argued that the Bible is divinely inspired, there is no doubt as to the influence of human beings on the words. The oldest surviving documents we have of the New Testament are written in Greek. There are some who are able to read Greek and use the original Greek manuscripts to study scripture, but the rest of us are forced to read the words of the Bible in translated form. The original Greek manuscripts were translated into Latin and for many years Latin was the official language of the church. Then Gutenberg developed the printing press and it allowed the Bible to be printed in mass. The printing press allowed the Bible to be translated into many languages. Go into any Christian bookstore, or any bookstore that sells Bibles, and you will see Bibles in multiple languages and multiple versions in the same language. In English, the most popular translations are the King James Version, New International Version, and English Standard.

With the dearth of Bible versions out there, can you honestly believe that all of them are the literal word of God? There are going to be some mistakes in the translations. There are going to be inconsistencies. There are going to be different interpretations of the original Greek words. These different interpretations won't affect the major points. God still created the universe. Adam and Eve are still the first people God created. Jesus is still the Son of God and gets crucified and is then resurrected. What changes are the small points. A small change in the syntax of a verse can lead to unintended contradictions, misinterpretations, and other problems. These are the reasons why it is difficult to defend the position of the Bible being the literal word of God. If it were the literal word of God, then it would be in the original Greek. Luckily for us, it is not confined to the Greek language and is open to people of all languages. God probably intended His word to be accessible to the world.

Although that may be the case, the Bible is not the complete history of human civilization. There is little written about the Roman Empire in the New Testament. The Old Testament briefly deals with the major ancient civilizations. The Egyptians take up a great part of the book of Exodus, but only from the point of view of the Israelites. There is no history of the development of Egypt or the history of Egypt after Moses leads the Israelites to freedom despite the influence Egypt held in the ancient Mediterranean world. The reason behind this is that the Old Testament is simply a history of God's chosen people – the Israelites. The New Testament features the Gospels, which tell the story of Jesus of Nazareth's life, and the history of the early Christian church, mainly told through the letters Paul of Tarsus wrote to churches around the Mediterranean. Everything else that was going on outside the Mediterranean world is not covered in the Bible. This simple reality of the Bible and its limitations tends to be obscured when evolutionists and creationists debate. The reason for this is the beginning of the Bible.

The Book of Genesis begins with the creation of the world and the first two people – Adam and Eve. This forms the crux of the evolution-creation debate. Can it be believed that God created the world in seven days? Is it true that Adam and Eve were the first two people? Were their offspring the first humans? If so, then there is a genealogy of humanity.

This genealogy only goes back several thousand years instead of the hundreds of thousands that scientists believe. Can the Bible and findings of scientists be reconciled? I don't believe so. I also don't believe that it matters.

To start, remember that the Bible is not meant to be the complete history of human civilization. There will be parts that are cut out. For instance, where are the dinosaurs? They are not included in the Bible because they have nothing to do with the history of the Israelites or early Christian church. That does not mean that dinosaurs did not exist. It just means that they aren't included in the Bible. The same is true with the prehistoric ancestors of humans. Creatures like homoerectus or the Neanderthals existed and are not included in the Bible because they had no ties to the Israelites.

What about God creating the world in seven days? I'm not an expert on what God can and cannot do. If the Book of Genesis records that God created everything in the universe in seven days then I have no reason to doubt it. We are dealing with an all-seeing, all-knowing, all-loving, and all-powerful God. Anything is possible. So the world that was created by God in seven days might not necessarily be the one that we inhabit now. It could have taken millions of years to cook, like scientists believe.

Now about Adam and Eve, were they the first two human beings? Was there actually a Garden of Eden? Traditionally, the Garden of Eden has been believed to lie in the Middle East between the Tigris and Euphrates Rivers. There is no such garden there at the present time. So where is this Garden of Eden if it actually exists? Perhaps it is heaven. Adam and Eve were created in God's image and lived with God in heaven, but got kicked out due to sin. If the Garden of Eden exists, then human beings haven't found it. Not that any of that matters. In fact, it doesn't matter if Adam and Eve were the first human beings.

There always has to be a first of anything. For the Israelites the first people were Adam and Eve. For scientists, the belief is that all human beings are descended from a woman in Africa. So the Garden of Eden is really in Africa? No. The Adam and Eve story does not have to be reconciled with the findings of science because all that really matters regarding the story is that the world was created by God and God created people. This is the argument creationists should be making in their debates with evolutionists because it is powerful.

Take a look around you and you will see humanity and its creations. Roads, parks, buildings, cars are all creations of human intellect. Human beings have created settlements around the globe. Humans have explored the oceans and the frozen continent of Antarctica. Humans have used telescopes to look at the stars, satellites to study the solar system, and explorers to take samples from the moon. Now think about some of the other developments made by human beings. There is the monetary system. Exchanging one item for another of equal value was an ancient practice. It has evolved over the years to encompass precious metals like gold and silver, paper money, and now it seems like money has become a set of digits on a computer or a plastic card that can be swiped. There are other abstract ideas such as philosophy, democracy, and even religion. The human mind has developed all of these throughout its brief time on this Earth. For what purpose? Think of the game of basketball. I enjoy playing and watching basketball, but I cannot tell you the evolutionary purpose of the game of basketball. I can, however, tell you that if we are created in God's image then there is a reason for the way we are. We have the intellect to develop the concept of democracy because God is intelligent. We can create scientific instruments that can explore the universe because God is a creator as well. We can even create and enjoy the game of basketball even though it doesn't appear to have any evolutionary purpose. We can do this because God takes joy in everything He does.

Now compare the accomplishments of humanity to those of the other species of the Earth. I was at the zoo and stood for five minutes watching a giraffe trying to eat a stick. He had the stick in his mouth horizontally, but not in such a way that he could tilt his head back and eat the stick. Instead, he rolled the stick over his teeth and around his mouth. Finally he got the stick placed in his mouth vertically. He chomped down and half the stick fell out of his mouth. The other half he was able to eat. He didn't look for the rest of his stick. Instead, he went back to the tree for another one. I couldn't believe that a creature that had been on this Earth for millions of years couldn't develop a brain large enough to figure out how to eat a whole stick. Perhaps there is no evolutionary benefit to a giraffe being able to eat a whole stick, but I doubt that.

Look around at the animal world though. Is there one animal out there that has created what humans have? Dolphins are considered among the most intelligent animals in the world. Have they created a spaceship and explored the moon? What about apes? Apes have been in space, but they got there because of human ingenuity. The blue whale has the largest brain of all mammals. Has an exploratory party of blue whales reached the coast to study humans? Dogs spend a great deal of time around human beings. Do they have a concept of religion? Cockroaches are some of the oldest creatures on Earth. Have they developed a transportation system that can take them over large distances like humans have with the airplane, automobile, train, and even covered wagon?

It is clear that humans are the superior animal on the planet. Consider global warming. The whole idea behind global warming is that human beings are so powerful that they are influencing the temperature of the Earth. Without human burning of fossil fuels and cultivating the land, the

Earth would not be under so much strain.

It is difficult to believe that after millions of years other animals have been unable to come close to matching the accomplishments of human beings. Something is wrong with evolution. However, if humans have been created in God's image, then the superiority of the human being is not so unbelievable. God would obviously make humans able to control the world He created. The achievements of human beings in science, philosophy, and any other endeavor occur because we are created in God's image.

This conclusion has been reached through simple observation of nature. Observation is one of the hallmarks of the scientific method. In fact, when Charles Darwin came up with his theory of evolution he was basing it on the observations he made on his travels. He was able to see the changes in different species of birds and how certain traits were going to be beneficial for the future of that species.

Darwin's theory of evolution is powerful. It gives a great explanation for the physical evolution of a species. It has spawned the science of anthropology where scientists have been able to trace the physical evolution of the human species. This physical evolution is most easily seen in the development of the human body. Humans have gotten taller with each generation. Go to a historical site from the 1800s and watch a six foot five inch adult try to get in the door. He will have to duck his head in order to enter. It is easy to draw conclusions like humans have naturally evolved from apes and other humanoids because of the physical and biological similarities of these creatures. Physically and biologically this makes sense, but the theory of evolution does not adequately provide explanations for the mental evolution of human beings.

Thousands of years ago humans painted in caves. Typically these paintings take the form of animals in the area. Sometimes there are human beings, normally drawn as stick figures, surrounding a large animal in a hunt. These cave paintings are described by anthropologists as being the first signs of artwork. There is some debate about what these paintings mean. Some believe they are religious paintings. The humans are paying homage to the spirit world and asking for help in the hunt by depicting their enemy on the cave wall. Others believe the paintings are a sort of playbook for attacking these gigantic animals. A human could have gathered his friends around the painting and then explained how they were going to attack their dinner.

Scientists are too concerned with answering the wrong why question. The issue isn't why these paintings were created. The question is why were they paintings? I am asking why the first human would develop the concept of painting. How did this person conceive of making paints and then putting this concoction on a wall?

To be clearer and closer to my point, my interest is in the first to do something. The first painter. The first speaker. The first writer.

Consider language. First there needs to be the concept of language. This is not difficult to see in early human beings. Human beings gathered together for protection and kinship. They would need a form of communication unless they just wanted to sit and stare at one another. They might start with gestures, but then they would have to move on to verbal communication. This is not quite as easy. For instance, if I want to tell someone who does not speak English to sit in a chair, I might gesture toward the chair. If they still don't understand the gesture then I might go over to the chair and demonstrate the act of sitting. If they still don't get it, then I would have to verbalize my wishes. I would go over to the chair and grab it and call it a chair. I would repeat the word chair over and over until it became clear that the person I was talking to understood what I meant. Luckily for me, the other person will have a native language, even if it is not English. He would reply by calling the chair whatever a chair is called in his native language. From that base, we could have a reasonable, if difficult, conversation. He would do his best to bridge the gap between his language and my language and I would do my best to make a similar bridge. But the first human beings did not have the benefit of multiple languages. They were creating language. So how did that work?

It is not like a parent teaching a child to speak. The child is younger and will look toward the parent for guidance. There will be no resistance. If I call a chair a chair a child will go along with that. They may call the chair a table for a few months as they try to distinguish between the two items, but eventually the child will come around and call a chair a chair because the English language has standardized a chair as a chair and not as a table.

If early human beings used this technique of teaching words to their children then each clan would have its own language. Perhaps this was the case and the only way that languages could change would be when one clan conquered the other. The clan that called a chair a table could be conquered by the clan that called a chair a chair and since the conquerors exerted control over the whole clan then everyone came to call a chair a chair. This is getting into the evolution of language though.

I want to return to the concept of the first. In the clan there would be the first person to call a chair a chair. If this person had some standing in the clan then he would be listened to and the others would go along with his term for chair and be able to communicate with one another that way. This is a reasonable explanation and fits in with the above idea of hegemony in the evolution of language. The issue of other firsts besides language is now raised. Is the first person who came up with the concept of language and the first person who came up with the idea of words and taught the rest of the clan the words also the first person who came up with the concept of writing or cave painting? I know these other concepts did not develop at the same time as verbal language, but the concept of the first is still raised here. In particular, if the first person to create language was the most powerful, then was the first person to develop painting the most powerful in another clan? Again, I am unsure of the answer and we are beginning to drift away from the crux of the evolution-creation argument.

Evolution and creationism are explanations for two different developments. Creationism is concerned with the creation of the first human beings. Evolution explains the development of humans over generations. Evolution does not deal with the first human. Somehow the first human being just appeared out of the womb of some woman in Africa and that started the process to get to where we are today.

Consider this explanation though. In actuality there could not be a first human being. There would have to be two to start a species. And there could not just be any two. There had to be a man and a woman. There had to be an Adam and Eve in order for the human species to grow and develop. Have evolutionists been able to provide an Adam and Eve? Well, there's that woman in Africa who is considered to be the woman every human being on the planet is originally descended from. There is no information about the male who impregnated her. Was he a Neanderthal? Was he also a human being? Was she even a human being?

The questions about the first human beings can continue but there are no answers. Scientists have been unable to tell us how exactly the first human beings came about. There might be no historical evidence available or that evidence might not have been found yet.

I am not a mathematician, so I cannot tell you the probability of what we now know as a human being being able to appear out of the womb of one woman in Africa hundreds of thousands of years ago. How many times was a male human created but died out because there was no female? Or vice-versa? Perhaps it really did take millions of years before nature was able to provide us with a male and female human being to start the species. However, the chance of that happening seems low. In fact, the chance for all of eveloution working out the exact way it has seems low.

To have some liquid develop into physical creatures over millions of years is just as unbelievable as God creating the world and humanity. In fact, the idea of liquid becoming physical creatures without some sort of help from an unseen power is just too great to believe.

Creationism provides the micro explanation for humanity's creation that evolution cannot provide. God created Adam and Eve in his image. We can look around at our world and see how superior human beings are compared to other animals. It is difficult to believe in the superiority of humans without some explanation, such as God creating us in His image.

3 SIN

Sin is one of the most difficult barriers to get over in order to believe in God. So much has been written and said about sin that it's difficult to know what sin is and is not. Televangelists will spend many Sundays preaching about the evils of humans and the need to repent for your sins. This is a difficult message for someone who is interested in learning more about God. On the one hand, Christians say God is all love. On the other, God will send you to eternal hell if you do not confess your sins. Which is correct?

Original sin is the term used to describe the fall of Adam and Eve from the Garden of Eden. God gave Adam and Eve one rule in the garden – do not eat from the Tree of Knowledge. A snake was able to convince Eve to take an apple from the tree to eat. The snake told Eve that the apple was the greatest fruit in the garden and that God did not have her and Adam's best interests at heart. So she believed the snake and took the apple to Adam. They ate and God kicked them out of the Garden of Eden for breaking His one rule. Due to this transgression, human kind has been unable to return to the Garden of Eden.

The story of Adam and Eve can cause many people to conclude that God doesn't exist and the Bible is all junk even if they are open to the possibility of there being some divine guide behind all of life. There are several reasons for the difficulty of the Adam and Eve story. To start, there is the idea that a snake is able to speak. I have never seen a talking snake. If I did, I would believe that I was hallucinating or dreaming. At the very least, I wouldn't take a talking snake's word as truth.

The explanation for the talking snake is that it is actually Satan in snake form talking to Eve. That's fine, but it still doesn't explain why Eve or anyone else would believe the words of a talking snake. If Eve had never seen a snake before then perhaps it would not be difficult for her to believe that snakes talk. Or perhaps Satan put Eve under some sort of spell so that she would take the apple to Adam. Of course if that were true then there would be no such thing as free will and it would be a mistake to kick Adam and Eve out of the Garden of Eden. But God doesn't make mistakes – humans do however.

A key tenet of sin is that it is committed by human beings possessing free will. We as humans are able to do what we want. If we want to run down the street naked during rush hour then we are free to do so. It might violate some social conventions and traffic laws, but nobody is going to prevent us from doing it. The same is true with something like murder. There will be consequences for the committing of murder, but nobody is going to be able to stop us from committing murder unless someone knows about the murder plot beforehand. So the argument that Satan put Eve under a spell holds no weight. Eve knew that it was wrong to eat from the Tree of Knowledge. She just felt that Satan's argument about God not having her and Adam's best interests at heart was true. God gave them free reign over the Garden of Eden except for the Tree of Knowledge. Wouldn't it make sense that He would horde the best fruit on the one tree that Adam and Eve could not eat from? Certainly we as humans would horde the best for ourselves. And if we are created in God's image then maybe He'd also do the same as us. Eve bought this argument and brought the apple to Adam. This is where the theological point of the Adam and Eve original sin story lies, just like the theological point of the creation story is in God creating the universe and creating human beings in His image.

Still, this explanation does little to clarify what sin is and why human beings are scarred by sin. Basically sin is going against God's will. Adam and Eve went against God's will, so they were kicked out of the Garden of Eden. This is one of the reasons why you hear preachers always talking about your going to hell if you continue to sin. Adam and Eve were punished for their sins and you will be too. At least, that's one way to look at sin. This is more of the radical view that is good for drawing media attention, but does little to help or entice converts to Christianity.

Sin is difficult to understand. It is an uncomfortable subject that we do not want to think about. It is also vitally important to believing in God. I did not fully understand sin until I read C.S. Lewis' *Mere Christianity*. In the book, Lewis presents a picture of God as perfection. As human beings, none of us are perfect, yet we all know what is perfect. Lewis' argument is that human beings understand the concept of perfection because God is perfect. If God is perfect and humans understand the concept of perfection, then that means God exists. There is no way for us to know what perfection is, yet never see it in our lives, unless something acts as a model for perfection. The model of perfection is God.

Let's look at the airline industry for a moment. Certainly the airline industry is not run perfectly. In fact, the disparity between the airline industry's conception of perfection and reality is a good example when thinking of humanity's conception of perfection and its reality. Each year the airline companies create their flight schedules. These flight schedules are designed to maximize the investments the companies have made in labor, aircraft, fuel, and all the other materials needed to run an airline. The flight schedules are fully booked with planes crisscrossing the country. The schedules are made with considerations only for the amount of time it usually takes a plane to fly in the air from one destination to the next and then a brief period so that the plane can be refueled, people can get on and off, and routine maintenance checks made.

Each and every winter these perfectly designed flight schedules fail. They fail because of the weather. The weather cannot be predicted. Snow bogs down the east coast or the Midwest and shuts down some of the country's major airports. This throws off the rest of the schedule for not only the remainder of the day, but also for multiple days in some cases. The people who make the flight schedules must know that weather with wreck havoc with their schedules, yet they do nothing to change them. The idea behind this is that if there are no weather problems then the schedule should go along perfectly. Even then, there are the usual human errors. If the passengers are slow deplaning or getting on or there is a problem with the baggage then the flights can run a few minutes late. A few minutes late might not be a big inconvenience to passengers, but a few minutes late is not perfect.

As we can see, the idea of perfection is ingrained in humanity. We just constantly fail to achieve that perfection. This relates to sin because sin can be looked at as our failure to live up to the perfection in our mind. Whenever you hear someone say that you are a sinner, your natural reaction is to say that you are not. When you hear someone say that you are not perfect, your natural reaction should be to agree with them. Otherwise, you will most likely make a mistake within the next five minutes and your belief in your own perfection will be proven wrong. Now obviously there are different degrees of mistakes. A typo is not the same as a terrorist attack. So the comparison between mistakes and sin is not completely correct, but it is a good starting point. It is difficult to say that you are a sinner because sin has taken on such a negative form today. It is a word full of fire and brimstone. On the other hand, there is perfection. If you say that you aren't perfect then you can live with that. Sin lies somewhere between making a typo and doing something that will land you in hell for eternity.

Take for example a mother who scolds her child for spilling the milk at breakfast. Who is the sinner here? Is it the child for spilling the milk? After all, the spilling of milk is a mistake. But it isn't a significant mistake. It is only spilled milk and not worth getting upset over. So the sin is committed by the mother. She may immediately regret the tone and words she used to scold her child over such an insignificant mistake. This is sin. The mother's anger is unwarranted. The same is true whenever you are in traffic and you curse out the driver who has cut you off. You may feel better after you have done the cursing, but it is unwarranted.

So does that mean that sin is just the mistakes that you regret making toward other people? The answer is no. There is more to it than that.

Essentially, sin is doing something that we know we should not do. Adam and Eve knew that they should not eat from the Tree of Knowledge. They did that and were punished for their transgression. The woman who scolds her child knows she should not take that type of tone with a mistake that is so insignificant. She repents by feeling bad. So how do we know that we are doing something we shouldn't? We can use the Bible as a guide. There are the Ten Commandments and what seems like hundreds of other rules. Those rules are difficult to remember, they also feel outdated at times, and who really wants to deal with a lot of rules anyway? Jesus was asked what is the key to life. He replied that all the rules of the Bible can be summed up by loving God and loving others. Treat others like you wish to be treated. This is a lot easier to remember, but it doesn't clarify the idea of sin.

How do we know that we are doing something we should not do? Let us return to C.S. Lewis' idea of perfection. We know inherently what perfection is because we are created in the image of God, who is perfect. If we know what perfection is, then we also know when we do not attain that perfection. Think of the airplane schedulers in the winter months. They know what a perfect flight schedule looks like. They also know what an imperfect flight schedule looks like once the weather turns poor. For that matter, every passenger in the airport also knows what a perfect flight schedule and an imperfect schedule looks like. So does that mean that the flight schedulers are sinners because they don't live up to perfect standards? No.

There is also the issue of free will. Adam and Eve chose to eat the fruit from the Tree of Knowledge. The mother chose to scold her child. Now the mother might have been acting out of anger and immediately regretted her tone, but that doesn't change the fact that she had the choice to scold or not to scold. The flight schedulers do not have free will in their case. They have free will in making the schedule, but they cannot control the weather. They cannot save the perfect flight schedule because of forces outside of their control. Therefore, what they have done is not a sin.

Basically free will means that we as human beings are able to do what we like. We are created in God's image. God is free to do what He likes. As humans, we are free to do what we want on Earth. That means we are free to love others or to hurt others. Free will is frequently cited as a reason for why there is human suffering in the world. It is also important in relation to sin. Human beings have the freedom to choose to sin.

Sometimes it isn't quite as black and white as having the freedom to choose to sin. Think of the mother from the example above. She sinned by taking her child to task over the spilled milk. She immediately regretted what she did. Her free will was impeded by anger. If she hadn't gotten angry then she wouldn't have chosen to yell at her child. So emotion also plays a role in human sin. Emotions are not meant to be an excuse for human sin. Emotions are what make life so enjoyable to live. And of course, we get our emotions from God.

God has emotions. God is full of love, but God also gets angry. The second half of the Old Testament is filled with God's anger. Was God's anger justified or was it sinful? It was certainly justified. God made a covenant with Abraham in the Old Testament. He told Abraham that he would have a race of people that would be as multiple as the stars in the sky or the sand on the beach. Abraham's people would be the Israelites. When Moses led the Israelites out of Egypt, God renewed the covenant. He said that He would be their God and the Israelites would be His people. Except the Israelites rejected God. They created a golden calf and worshiped that as a thanks for getting them out of Egypt. In retaliation, God let the Israelites walk around for forty years in the wilderness. It was only after everyone who lived in Egypt had died that God allowed the Israelites access to the land he promised.

The Old Testament is filled with stories of the Israelites rejecting God in favor of some other idol. God endowed human beings with free will, so the Israelites were able to reject Him in favor of other idols. That does not mean that they wouldn't face punishment for their actions. It just means that God allowed them to do what they wished. It is just like the social mores, laws, and other rules that we have in modern society. People are free to do what they like, but if they break a law then they will have to face consequences. In the case of the Israelites, when they rejected God, they were left to their own devices. This led them to slavery in Egypt, wandering around in the wilderness, and eventually they were conquered by the Babylonians. Each time they suffered they cried out to God for help. God answered their calls each and every time. Despite their rejecting Him, despite their sinning, each and every time God came back to them because He is full of love.

It is difficult not knowing what for sure is considered sinful or not. What is justifiable anger? What is a mistake that can be forgiven? Well, know that you are free to make mistakes. As a human you will make mistakes. We're imperfect. However, also understand that God is perfect and cannot tolerate mistakes. He will forgive you for your mistakes because He is love, but do not blatantly commit a crime or hurt someone because

God will get angry and make you pay. Just think of the Israelites who left Egypt and wandered around in the wilderness for forty years.

Let's return to Adam and Eve again. Adam and Eve were kicked out of the Garden of Eden because of their sin. Sin was transferred to the rest of the human race by that one action of Adam and Eve. Essentially all humanity has been punished because of the mistake of someone who we have never met before. For the longest time this idea made it difficult for me to believe in God. I couldn't understand how an omnibenevolent God could hold a grudge against humanity for a mistake made by one ancestor living long ago. I also couldn't understand why the people in the Bible didn't curse Adam and Eve at every opportunity for passing along their original sin to everybody else. If Adam and Eve hadn't made the first mistake then we would not be capable of sin. However, we are capable of sin.

Luckily for us, God is benevolent. He told Adam and Eve to leave Eden because of their sin, but He also decided to go with them into the world. He did not abandon them even though they sinned. The same is true for you and me. He has not abandoned us because he sent his son, Jesus of Nazareth to suffer for our sins. Now you may not be completely sure about sin and Adam and Eve and now Jesus dying for our sins, but think of it as a simple one for one trade. Adam and Eve committed original sin. Jesus' death atoned for our sins. Adam and Eve were the original sinners. Jesus' death saves us from sin. This is why you do not see any bitterness today over Adam and Eve for making us sinners. We are saved if we believe that Jesus is the Son of God and he died for our sins. God gave us the free will to believe in Jesus as the forgiver of sins. This is why there is a focus on Jesus in Christianity. It is because of Jesus that we are made right with God.

Jesus is the cornerstone of the Christian religion. Unfortunately, there are a growing number of people who want to believe that Jesus of Nazareth never existed. As esoteric as sin or even creationism can be, there is no doubt that Jesus of Nazareth existed. The historicity of Jesus of Nazareth is explored in the next chapter.

4 THE HISTORICAL JESUS

The Old Testament prophets believed that a savior would be sent by God to save the Israelites from oppression. Christians believe that Jesus of Nazareth is God's Chosen One. In Hebrew the term is Messiah. In Greek, it is Christos. In English, this is translated into Christ. Therefore, Jesus of Nazareth is frequently referred to as Jesus Christ in Christian texts.

Unfortunately, there has been a push against Christians from atheists revolving around questions of Jesus' existence. Too bad for the atheists that through reason and logic the case is pretty clear that Jesus of Nazareth really existed. It is only a small leap of faith that is needed to believe that Jesus really is who he said he is – the Son of God, the Savior, the Messiah, the Christ.

Now the first strike against the atheist argument comes from history. In particular, there is no historical writing against Christianity that questions the existence of Jesus. It would be a gigantic blow against the developing Christian faith if detractors could point out that Jesus never existed. But there is no evidence that this happened. So if people writing closer to the first century, not 2,000 years later like atheists, were unable to provide proof or arguments against the historical Jesus, then how are modern critics able?

Their argument usually revolves around the lack of evidence *for* the historical Jesus. They like to question the Biblical authors and how the Bible developed over hundreds of years. The historicity of the Bible and its authors will be discussed in the next chapter. For now, it is sufficient to say that the greatest source of the existence of the historical Jesus comes from the first four books of the New Testament. These are called the Gospels. They tell the story of Jesus' life and deeds.

Outside of the Gospels, Jesus does not often appear in writings from around the first century. He clearly appears in a great deal of writings from the fourth century on once Rome became a Christian empire. This doesn't make sense. If Jesus was the Son of God, if he was the Savior, if he did all sorts of amazing deeds like raising people from the dead, if he really was a great teacher, then wouldn't there be more written about him?

This question holds a lot more weight today. Literacy rates were low in the first century. The Roman Empire was vast and there was not a great deal of interest by the Romans in establishing schools in the territories they controlled. An educated populace might get ideas about rebellion. It is estimated that about ten percent of the population in the Roman Empire was literate. The majority who were literate typically were involved in the religious world. They were either the major priests in Jerusalem or one of the local rabbis (another word for teacher) who would lead religious gatherings in the towns dispersed around Israel. Some scholars doubt that Jesus of Nazareth was literate. Although this is difficult to believe because of the depth of Jesus' knowledge of the Old Testament. He would have been able to learn the scriptures from a local rabbi. The rabbi would read from hand printed scrolls and he would teach the young Jesus how to read the scrolls. Of course this is assuming that Jesus was just a historical person. If Jesus really was the Son of God then there is no doubt as to his ability to read and write.

So if Jesus was a great teacher, then wouldn't it have made sense for him to write down all of his teachings and then they would be preserved for future generations? That might make sense from our mindset. We are used to the relative ease with which books and writings can be printed and distributed. With the Internet this is done instantly. Prior to the Internet, books could be bound and shipped across the world in massive quantities. But those capabilities didn't occur until Joseph Guttenberg invented the printing press. So if Jesus were to just write down his teachings then he would have only reached ten percent of the population. And the majority of the population who read were those religious teachers who had Jesus killed because they did not like what he said about them.

Each and every scroll had to be handwritten in the first century. It took time to copy everything by hand. There are also the inherent mistakes that humans make when transcribing.

Instead, Jesus lived in a society in which stories and traditions and teachings were passed down through generations via words. The oral tradition as it has been termed by scholars. The oral tradition plays a big part in determining the historicity of the Bible. Jesus' reliance on verbal teachings that would be remembered by his followers so that they could pass along his message after his death is completely consistent with what we know about the oral tradition. If Jesus were a concoction by Romans in the fourth century or later then there should be hints and clues that he taught and lived like someone in fourth century Rome, but there is no evidence for this conclusion.

Still, the Gospels cannot be completely taken as unbiased testimony of Jesus' life. They were obviously written to spread the word of Jesus. This purpose needs to be remembered. It is a point that Biblical scholars continually drive home. So the bias of the Gospels just means that further evidence might need to be consulted.

Unfortunately, there are little other written reports of Jesus or his deeds from around the first century. This is not unusual however. The majority of people living in the first century have no written records of their existence. The Romans did not have complete records. Or at least, we have not found their records. Perhaps a Roman census or the tax collecting records will eventually be found, but for now there is little physical evidence available of individuals living in the first century.

In fact, there is little evidence for the existence of important people like Pontius Pilate. Pilate is best known as being the Roman prefect who ordered Jesus' crucifixion. Yet, the most we know about him comes from the Bible. He is mentioned a few times in the Jewish historian Josephus' history of the Jewish people. There was a plaque found in Israel that stated Pilate's official title was prefect, but otherwise there is little that we know about this man. Pilate was the top Roman official in Jerusalem.

Jerusalem was not a major city in the Roman Empire, but it was still important because of how different it was from the rest of the Empire. While other conquered peoples would readily adapt to Roman customs, the Jews in Israel were resistant. They would continue to worship their God and observe their customs even under Roman oppression. In 66 C.E. a group of zealous Jews led an armed rebellion against Roman oppression. The rebellion ended up costing the Jews severely. In 70 C.E. the Temple in Jerusalem was destroyed by the Romans. Nearly all the Zealots who rebelled were either killed by Roman soldiers or committed suicide.

Since Jerusalem was such a difficult area to maintain, the position of prefect was not highly prized by aspiring Roman bureaucrats. For many years, Herod the Great ruled over all of Israel. He was half Jewish and made a few attempts to placate his subjects. He is the one who made the Temple in Jerusalem one of the most magnificent man-made wonders of the ancient world. Otherwise, he was a Roman through and through. He was brutal to his people, including family members. He had several of his family members murdered because he was afraid they might attempt to take his throne. However, another of his major accomplishments was the creation of the port city of Caesarea on the Mediterranean. Cesaria was named for Caesar Augustus, the man who put Herod the Great on the throne.

Paying tribute to the emperor was one of the ways Roman bureaucrats used to rise in the organization. Unfortunately for Herod the Great, he died before he could leave Israel. His kingdom was divided into three parts. Two of his sons controlled the upper and lower regions of Israel. The upper region was known as Galilee. Nazareth was one of the cities in Galilee. Fortunately, we know a great deal about Galilee in the ancient world. The Jewish historian Josephus was also from Galilee. He fought and chronicled the uprising against Rome in the late first century. His experiences fighting Romans in Galilee are used to influence his history of the Jewish uprising and of the Jewish people as a whole.

Josephus confirms that Pilate was given control of Judea, the middle part of Israel, in which Jerusalem lay. If there was a prime position to rule in Israel, then it was Judea. Jerusalem was the largest city in Israel and Judea was the most populous province. Pilate received this job because his wife was related to the emperor. Like in modern times, nepotism was the surest way to get ahead. So if Pilate were not related to the emperor, and if he didn't play such a large part in the Jesus story, then all we would know about him would be what was written by Josephus.

Josephus was not kind to Pilate. He characterizes Pilate as a dictator. Pilate was quick to anger and not afraid to use force when angry. Josephus' characterization cannot be dismissed as that of an enemy combatant against a rival. There is probably some merit. Soon after the crucifixion of Jesus, Pilate was recalled to Rome. There is no reason given for this recall, but Josephus speculates that it was because of Pilate's treatment of his subjects. Of course the replacements for Pilate could not have been any better if the Jews rebelled against the Romans thirty years later. Whatever the reason, as soon as Pilate leaves Judea, he is no longer heard from.

The point here is that Pilate was once the ruler of a province in the Roman world. Not many people aspired to or could hold such a position. Through his marriage he was able to get this post. If he hadn't been placed as the head of a province, then there is a good chance that he would have nothing written about him. The fact that Josephus wanted to preserve the history of the Jews, and the Gospel writers wanted to preserve the deeds of Jesus, allow Pilate's name to be remembered in history. Otherwise, he'd just be a brief name on a plaque found in the twentieth century. Most people wouldn't even have a plaque with their name on it. Instead, they would have died with no knowledge of their having existed except through family members. So it should come as no surprise that little outside of the Gospels is written about Jesus. He was a teacher from a non-descript town in Galilee. At the time, there were supposedly plenty of other teachers and prophets who could cast out demons and do miracles. Jesus was not spectacular enough to warrant people writing stories about him. Or was he?

Since Josephus is considered the authority of Jewish history in the first century then he should be consulted first. Jesus makes two appearances in Josephus' two books. This can be looked at as not a great deal of appearances, especially since Jesus was supposed to be the Messiah. Jesus was the Messiah for those who believed in him. For a Jew like Josephus, he was nothing more than a teacher from Galilee. Therefore, Jesus would not make many appearances in Josephus' history of the Jewish people or the war with Rome at the end of the first century because he did not impact either.

The most useful example from Josephus is when Jesus appears in relation to his brother, James. James is mentioned as being killed. He is referred to in the passage as the brother of Jesus (See Josephus's *Antiquities of the Jews* Book 20, Chapter 9). Some translations of the passage include a sentence fragment about Jesus also being called the Christ, but this was most likely added later. James was a common name in first century Israel. There were two other James' among the twelve disciples of Jesus. Since James was such a common name it makes sense that this James would be given some distinction. This was usually done by listing where the person was from.

For instance, take Judas Iscariot. Judas was also a common name in first century Israel. The name comes from Judas Maccabee, a great warrior for the Jewish people who led a revolt against the Seleucid Empire in 167-160 B.C.E. Once Rome took over, the name Judas was given to sons in honor of the rebellious warrior. So Judas needed some distinction from the other Judas' in the Bible, one of them also being a follower of Jesus who went by the nickname of Thaddeus. Jesus even had a brother named Judas. Therefore, Judas, the one who betrays Jesus, is referred to by where he comes from. Iscariot means man from Kerioth. The name gives Judas a distinction. It also points out that he is an outsider. The rest of Jesus' disciples came from Galilee. Kerioth is a town in the southern part of Judea.

But Josephus does not refer to James by where he is from. Instead, Josephus decides to refer to James through his brother. Family members were usually reserved for women, who are referred to as wife or mother of a man (Mary, wife of Joseph), or young men, such as when son of is used to describe someone (James, son of Zebedee). Now Jesus would have been more famous than James. In fact, Jesus is the first one mentioned in the passage. Josephus starts by mentioning that the brother of Jesus was brought before the authorities. Then he goes on to name the brother of Jesus as James. There are also some other men who were with James. These men, James and the others, were brought before the authorities because they were law breakers. The law breakers were then delivered to be stoned.

It was against Jewish custom to execute someone. This is why Jesus had to be brought before Pilate. Pilate had to agree to the crucifixion in order to placate his subjects, Jewish priests who felt that Jesus was a blasphemer. However, the Jewish priests were allowed to stone people rather than condemning them to crucifixion. Stoning has a history in the Hebrew Bible. For instance, if a woman is caught as an adulterer, then she could have been stoned. Another crime punishable by stoning was blasphemy. Josephus indicates that the authorities who ordered James' stoning were the Jewish priests. They could only stone James if he committed blasphemy. And he could only commit blasphemy if he believed in something other than the word of the Jewish priests. Believing in Jesus as the Messiah would be grounds for blasphemy. Therefore, it makes sense that Josephus starts his story by mentioning Jesus and then building up to the death of Jesus' brother James.

Josephus includes this story because the head priest who ordered the stoning was new. This was a newsworthy event. It was like the first bill signing by a new president. It would be worth preserving for posterity. It just happened to be that the man who the new head priest had stoned was the brother of Jesus. Josephus was not expecting his words to be used as proof of Jesus being the Messiah because Josephus did not believe Jesus was the Messiah. However he does know that Jesus is more important than James, which is why Jesus is mentioned first. Also that James' blasphemy is due to belief in Jesus would not happen if there was no Jesus to start Christianity.

Testimonium Flavianium

Testimonium Flavianium, the testimony of Flavius Josephus, is considered a forgery by most scholars. I tend to also believe this although there are parts of the passage that could be authentic. Most likely though, the juiciest parts that Christians cite over and over are forgeries that were entered in the fourth century when the Roman Empire became Christian.

The testimony appears in Book 18, Chapter 3, of *Antiquities of the Jews*. This was the book Josephus wrote to chronicle the history of the Jewish people. The translation by Louis H. Feldman in the Loeb Classical Library version of the book will be quoted in its entirety so that it can be broken down and shown how it is false.

"About this time there lived Jesus, a wise man, if indeed one ought to call him a man. For he was one who performed surprising deeds and was a teacher of such people as accept the truth gladly. He won over many Jews and many of the Greeks. He was the Messiah. And when, upon the accusation of the principal men among us, Pilate had condemned him to a cross, those who had first come to love him did not cease. He appeared to them spending a third day restored to life, for the prophets of God had foretold these things and a thousand other marvels about him. And the tribe of the Christians, so called after him, has still to this day not disappeared."

On the positive side, Josephus uses the word Messiah rather than Christ. Jesus is also referred to as a wise man. The Gospels are filled with people who are willing to acknowledge that Jesus was a wise man but not necessarily the Messiah. This is similar to those in our own time who will concede that Jesus was a wise teacher, but are not willing to go the whole way by calling him the Son of God. Josephus also mentions that Jesus was crucified by Pilate. Finally, Josephus states that Jesus' followers did not go away even after his death.

Now for the numerous problems with this testimony. To start, there is the issue of Jesus being the Messiah. Josephus flatly rejected this and would not have included it in his writing. Further proof of this passage being revised is that Jesus won over many Jews and Greeks. This is false. Nowhere in the Gospels does Jesus convert a group of Greeks. He is strictly teaching to the Jews. It isn't until Jesus is resurrected that he tells his disciples to spread the word of God to all nations. In particular, the apostle Paul is used to spread the word to the Greeks. Finally, there is the statement that the prophets had foretold of the deeds Jesus would perform. Although Christians do believe this, there would be no reason for a Jew like Josephus to believe Jesus' coming was foretold by the prophets. The Jews were expecting a warrior in the mode of King David who would overthrow Roman oppression. Instead they got a teacher from Nazareth.

If Josephus did write about Jesus then he probably stuck to the facts. Jesus was a wise teacher who was crucified by Pilate and still had followers after his death. This also fits in with what he wrote about James. The style is pure fact without excess commentary included.

Roman Sources

What about the followers of Christ in Rome? In 64 C.E. a great fire broke out in Rome. The Emperor Nero is believed to have started the fire, although recent scholarship has put some doubt into this theory because the reason people first believed for his starting the fire doesn't exactly fit with the facts of the fire. The actual cause of the fire does not matter. What matters is that Nero attempted to blame the start of the fire on Christians. In fact, Nero was known as a persecutor of Christians. The majority of our information about Nero's reign in Rome comes from Tacitus, writing around 110 C.E. Tacitus is the one who presents the theory that Nero attempted to blame the fire on Christians.

Now a common argument for those against the historicity of Jesus is that all of our writings, even the Gospels, are dated from the fourth century when Rome was a Christian empire. What of this action by Nero chronicled by Tacitus in the early second century? Obviously Christians had to be a significant amount of the population if they were going to be blamed for a fire that destroyed most of Rome. Therefore, there were plenty of believers only thirty years after Jesus' death. In fact, the stories of Jesus must have spread quickly for them to move from Israel along the Mediterranean coast to Rome.

Since Christians believed Jesus was the Son of God and they believed that there was one God, there would be major problems for them in the polytheistic culture of Rome. They would be easy targets for persecution. From what Tacitus describes, Nero enjoyed persecuting Christians. Now if Jesus were not an actual person, why would anyone defend him or be willing to die for him? It would be a lot easier to renounce Jesus as someone who was made up and go on believing in the Roman gods. It just doesn't make any sense. If human beings have a natural instinct toward self-preservation, as evolutionists say, then it would be natural that they renounce their beliefs in Jesus, especially if he were not real. Yet that wasn't the case. Christians continued to die for their beliefs. Jesus' own brother is an example in Jerusalem. Of course the fact that Jesus had a brother might be proof of his existence. On the other hand, there are those who might say that Jesus was just given a brother in order to make a stronger case for him being real. But why would the Son of God need a brother to prove his existence? Again, there is no good answer presented by those who doubt Jesus existed. It all makes sense though if Jesus did exist and people did believe that he was the Son of God.

There is further evidence of problems early Christians caused the Roman Empire. Around 112 C.E., Pliny the Younger, a magistrate in what is now modern Turkey, wrote a letter to the Roman Emperor Trajan, asking the emperor for help in dealing with Christians. Pliny writes that he forcibly required Christians to renounce Jesus. These Christians had been brought before him by anonymous accusers. Their one reason for being brought before him was because they were Christian.

Pliny the Younger was a prodigious writer. His uncle, Pliny the Elder, was a historian. What we know about Rome at the time of the great empire comes from historians like Pliny the Younger, Pliny the Elder, and Tacitus listed above. Scholars regard their writings to be authentic. Therefore, they can be used as further evidence that Jesus existed.

Pliny the Younger wrote in modern Turkey during the first century. That means that Christians were in existence in another region of the Mediterranean at an earlier time period than the fourth century when Rome became a Christian empire. Once again, Pliny points out the issues the local authorities and citizens were having with Christians. The Christian population was large enough to cause the authorities problems. This is less than a hundred years after Jesus died. Finally, there is the problem of Christians being tortured and not renouncing Jesus. There certainly were those who did renounce Jesus, but there were others who did not. Pliny wrote to Trajan to ask what he should do with the Christians brought before him who have not renounced Jesus despite being tortured. Pliny did not like having to execute them because their only crime was being Christian. If Jesus didn't exist then it would be easy to renounce him. But not everybody did. They didn't do it in Rome under Nero. They didn't do it in Turkey under Pliny. Why would they do this unless Jesus did exist and he really was the Son of God?

Remaining in Turkey, the leader of the church in Hierapolis was a man named Papias. Papias died sometime around 100 C.E. It is quite possible that some of the people he knew were persecuted by Pliny the Younger. Some of the other people he knew were John, the writer of the Gospel Book of John. Papias referred to John as John the Elder. He also knew several of the New Testament books. Now Papias will be discussed in greater detail in the next chapter, but he is mentioned here as further evidence of there being a strong Christian community in the Mediterranean long before Rome became a Christian empire under Constantine.

There are other religious sources that further the proof of Jesus' existence. One is from the Koran, the most holy book in the Islamic religion. Jesus is referred to in the Koran as a prophet from God, but not the Son of God. There are also some who read the Talmud, an ancient scroll used as a supplement to the Hebrew Bible, who believe that Jesus is referenced several times. But like in the Koran, Jesus is not mentioned by name. He is given other names, which decrease the authenticity of these sources in my mind.

So Jesus the person existed because he is mentioned in several ancient sources outside of the four Gospels. You can concede that now, but did he really start the Christian religion? What about Paul? Paul of Tarsus was known as Saul prior to his conversion to Christianity. The story goes that Saul persecuted Christians in Jerusalem shortly after Jesus' death. Then Jesus blinded him for three days and suddenly Saul became Paul, the man who Jesus tapped to spread his word to those living outside the Jewish world.

Paul takes on large importance to those who doubt the existence of Jesus because Paul's letters are considered to be the earliest surviving Christian documents. What intrigues those who don't believe Jesus existed is that Paul rarely mentions the historical Jesus. This is intriguing on the surface, but meaningless when looked at closer. Paul wrote several letters to churches around the Mediterranean. Some of these letters have been included in the New Testament. For instance, Paul wrote letters to the church in Corinth. These letters were designed to encourage the churches to further their faith. Paul provides guidelines on how the churches should conduct business and worship and how the congregation members should act.

Little is mentioned about Paul's own background or the historical Jesus in these letters. This makes sense though. Paul was writing to a group of believers. The members of the churches he wrote to already knew about Jesus. They'd heard the stories and they believed Jesus was the Son of God.

Why would Paul need to write about the historical Jesus in great detail then? He would have just wasted good parchment and time by beating a dead horse. Therefore, there is no good reason for why Paul should have written about the historical Jesus. He did not expect his letters to be collected and included in something called the New Testament. If he had the foresight to know that then maybe he would have written more about the historical Jesus. The style of his letters matches the reasoning behind their purpose, not some phony purpose someone living today wishes they had.

Despite the evidence above, there will still be those who deny Jesus existed. They'll find a way to weasel out of each of the historically documented examples of Jesus' existence mentioned above. Better yet, they'll have objections to stories about Jesus. These normally take the form of Jesus being no different from other pagan gods that are resurrected or the miracles of Jesus. How can you believe that a man can cast out demons (are those even real?), be born to a virgin, and come back from the dead?

Dating back to the nineteenth century, a popular belief among those who doubted the historicity of Jesus was that he was just another in a long line of pagan gods born on December 25 who died and rose from the dead. The December 25 part was abandoned as soon as it became clear that Jesus was not born December 25, but rather in the spring. December 25 is Christmas, the celebration of Jesus' birthday by Christians, because the Roman Empire wished to get rid of their pagan winter solstice festival once they converted to Christianity.

Many pagan religions believed that their god would die and then rise from the dead. Christians hold the same to be true of Jesus. Like the residents of Israel in the first century, these pagan religions were also based in agricultural societies. So the sun god would die and rise again based on the seasons. Jesus is only said to have risen once. Of course this can be explained away as a Jewish derivation on the standard sun god story. This argument would go that since the Jews were being ruled by the Romans, and the Romans controlled most of the Mediterranean, then there would be a great deal of cultural and religious mixing. That might be true, but the Jewish people have a long history of being ruled by foreign peoples, yet keeping their own beliefs and traditions. They were in Egypt until Moses brought them to the promised land. They were conquered by the Babylonians and then the Persians. Then came the Romans. Throughout all this, the Jews kept to their religious principles and did not change them to the preferences of their rulers. In this way, the Jews are different than a lot of other peoples conquered by the various major civilizations of the ancient western hemisphere.

But weren't the first followers of Jesus Jewish? Why did they convert if they stayed so true to Jewish beliefs? Perhaps because Jesus was real and who he said he was.

Osiris

There is one god in particular who always seems to be compared to Jesus. This is the Egyptian god of the dead – Osiris. Like Jesus, Osiris was said to have died and be resurrected. He also performed amazing deeds. He could have been a model for Jesus since there were Jews in Egypt. The Gospels also state the Jesus lived in Egypt for a short time when he was young. There are problems however. To start, even though there was still a Jewish population in Egypt, they didn't start the Jesus stories. Those stories started in Galilee.

There are other issues with the Osiris and Jesus comparisons. Osiris did die in a brutal way, just like Jesus. Except Osiris was cut into pieces and his body was spread to the corners of the Earth. No such story or belief has come about surrounding Jesus. Then there is the issue of Osiris' resurrection. Osiris wasn't exactly resurrected. His body was put together and he was given charge of the underworld. Jesus actually rose from the dead and appeared on Earth prior to his accession to heaven.

So Osiris is not a good comparison with Jesus. But could Osiris have influenced the Jesus story? Perhaps. A better explanation might be that since their creation, human beings have strived to understand the world around them. They could explain it through stories about sun gods or multiple gods like in Ancient Egypt, Greece, or Rome. Jesus could just be another variation in this explanation of the world around us.

Is Christianity the right view?

One of my biggest stumbling blocks was why is the Christian view the right view? Why isn't the Ancient Roman or Greek view the way the world is? Or even Islam or Judaism? Here is how I came about it that Christianity can be the only true religion.

Let's start with atheism. Atheists believe there is no divine being and that everything can be explained through natural processes. That's fine and good. There is a great deal about the world that we do not know. There is a great deal about ourselves that we do not know. This goes for physical and mental processes. We rarely understand why we make the decisions we do. We try to reason it out. Think of a relationship breakup. They are always difficult to go through. If you are the one doing the breaking-up, then you have to reason out to the best of your abilities why you wish to break-up with the other person. Perhaps there is a legitimate reason, such as an abusive relationship. Other times it just isn't clear. Two people drift away from each other. This experience is difficult to figure out. We have problems verbalizing our feelings when we drift apart from another person. We feel that we are distant from them, but how is that expressed in a nice way? If you are lucky, the other person feels the same as you. But that does not excuse you from going through the rationalization process of trying to figure out the exact moment and reason for why you have drifted apart.

Additionally, throughout human history there have been religious beliefs. How did this come about? The typical excuse is that early humans were not as sophisticated as we are today. This supposes that we are somehow superior to the humans who lived in previous centuries. Sure we might be able to design complex computers to help drive our cars and have sophisticated societies with traffic patterns, but at the most basic we're still human beings. We still make stupid mistakes (like leaving a cup of coffee on the top of our car) and still have the age old wants of food, drink, warmth, shelter, and love. These haven't changed over thousands of years. Neither has our belief in religion. Therefore, there has to be some truth to religion being necessary to humans. Scientists have theorized that there is a "God gene." This makes sense if there is a God. He'd want to include something like the "God gene" in his creations. It is up to us to choose which god is right, hence the proliferation of different religions over the years.

So, what about other religions? Let's start with the massive amount of polytheistic religions. These include the pagan religions and Hinduism. Now, in polytheistic religions there is a god for just about everything. There is a god of love, food, music, and so on. These gods have a specific specialty in which they command. In America we have something similar. We call them politicians. Some are more experienced in foreign affairs and are looked at as experts in this area. Others are teachers and are consulted on education. Now, do these politicians get along? No. If the world were inhabited with multiple gods then it probably would be closest to what the Ancient Greeks believed with the gods interfering and meddling in the lives of human beings in order to spite their rival gods. It would also be difficult to come to a consensus. There would be gods who want the sky to be green and others would like the sky to be blue. If the sky god were overthrown by a group of rivals, perhaps the sky would be green for a few days until the sky god regained control. We don't see that however. Therefore, it is hard to believe in a polytheistic world.

There are three major monotheistic religions in the world: Christianity, Judaism, and Islam. Christianity is an off-shoot of Judaism. Christians believe Jesus of Nazareth is the Messiah. His first followers were Jewish. After his death, the belief in a single god and Jesus being the Chosen One by God was spread to non-Jews. Jews are still waiting for their Messiah to spread the word of God to the masses. Unfortunately for them, it doesn't look like that is going to happen. While the Jews have waited for a Messiah, Jesus arrived. Jews in the first century wanted a Messiah who would overthrow Rome. Jesus did so in the fourth century when Constantine converted to Christianity. It might not have been on the schedule of those who hoped for immediate satisfaction, but it still doesn't take away from the fact that a Jew did overthrow the Roman Empire. Additionally, the word of God has been spread throughout the world by Christians. Christianity is currently the world's largest religion with over one billion believers.

The second largest religion in the world is Islam. Muslims believe in one god, named Allah. He is the same God that the Christians and Jews worship. Their major prophet is Mohammed. Mohammed believed that he was the true prophet of God. Even though Jesus, the main prophet of Christianity, and Moses, the main prophet of Judaism, were sent by God, Mohammed was the final prophet and was the one who would bring God's teachings to the masses. This may be true, but there is one major flaw that has continued to plague Islam to this day. In the Old Testament, Moses had a successor. Joshua was the one who brought the Israelites into the Promised Land after God got mad at his chosen people for worshiping a Golden Calf once they became free from Egyptian oppression. As punishment, the Israelites had to wander in the wilderness for forty years until everyone in the generation that sinned greatly was dead. This included Moses. But Moses was given a successor so that the Israelites would have a leader when they entered the Promised Land and had to fight with the land's occupants.

Jesus also had a successor. In fact, he had twelve of them. There were the eleven disciples Jesus originally chose, Judas Iscariot was the twelfth but he died soon after he betrayed Jesus. Additionally, there was Paul of Tarsus. Paul became a successor after Jesus died. Paul brought the word of Jesus to the non-Jews of the Mediterranean. Jesus' main disciple, Peter, was in charge of spreading the teaching of Jesus to the Jews. In fact, Jesus spent most of his public ministry teaching and preparing his disciples to spread his word among the masses.

Compare this to what happened after Mohammed died. He had no clear successor. He didn't appoint one. He didn't spend his time teaching and preparing his followers to spread his word. Instead, there was a battle for who would become head of his followers. Eventually there became two groups of Mohammed followers. One became known as the Sunnis. The other are the Shiite. They continue to bicker back and forth about which is the true successor to Mohammed. Now, if Mohammed really was the true prophet of God, then wouldn't God have chosen a successor for him like He did for Moses and Jesus? It just doesn't make sense that God would let it turn to chance or human intervention to determine a successor. That's not the way God appears to work. If Moses had a successor and Jesus had a successor, then Mohammed should have had a clear successor. Because Mohammed lacked a clear successor, it's difficult to put a lot of faith in Islam.

Christian Problems

There are certainly problems with the Jesus story. For instance, there is the issue of the virgin birth, resurrection, and all that talk about God and sin that would be much more pleasant if Jesus were just a wise teacher and not someone who claimed to be the Son of God. Let's start with the virgin birth. There is no explanation for the biology other than God is capable of inseminating a virgin in the way described in the Bible. It should be pointed out that after the insemination, Mary incubated Jesus for the requisite nine months like you'd expect from a typical pregnancy. Jesus then grew up in the typical human manner. He did not spring from Mary's womb as a thirty-year-old man ready to preach and teach.

More interestingly, there is the contradiction in the Jesus birth stories. Luke and Matthew both write about the birth of Jesus. They state that he was born to Mary and born in Bethlehem. Being born in Bethlehem is important. In the Old Testament, God taught the Israelites a lesson by letting the Babylonians come into the Promised Land and take over the area. Slowly, each of the Israelite cities fell. One of them was Bethlehem. It is pointed out that even though Bethlehem would fall to foreigners and was regarded as being insignificant, that one day the Messiah would be born there. Luke and Matthew take different routes to getting Jesus to Bethlehem though. Matthew doesn't say much about how Mary and Joseph get to Bethlehem. It can be assumed that they lived there originally in Matthew's tale. Although that does make it difficult when later on Jesus is referred to as being from Nazareth in Galilee. Matthew doesn't explain the reason for why Jesus is born in Bethlehem, yet is considered to be from Nazareth. Perhaps Mary and Joseph moved to Nazareth shortly after Jesus was born and he was raised there. Or perhaps Matthew was just trying to force Jesus' being born in Bethlehem so he'd fit with what the prophets predicted about the Messiah.

Luke makes it a point that Mary and Joseph are from Nazareth. They are required to go to Bethlehem in order to be counted for a census. Joseph is descended from the line of King David, who was born in Bethlehem, therefore, Joseph's family must return to Bethlehem in order to be counted. This is a stretch as well. Having people travel to their ancestral home is quite difficult. It is unlikely that members of an agricultural society would move off their farms to their ancestral homes just to be counted. Besides, there is no record of the census that was allegedly taken at the time of Jesus' birth. However, there is a census that was ordered in 6 C.E. following the death of Herod the Great. But Luke makes it clear that Jesus was born while Herod was still on the throne.

Now here is a possibility. Nazareth was a small town. Only about two or three extended families composed the town. Everyone would know each other. That means that everyone would know that Mary and Joseph were not married. If Mary started to show that she was pregnant and she was not married to Joseph, then she could legally be stoned to death. Although family members might not stoop to this measure, there certainly would have been a lot of unhappy relatives. Since Joseph had ties to Bethlehem, Luke's genealogy shows that Joseph was descended from King David, then it makes sense that Joseph would flee Nazareth for Bethlehem where he would know some of the people and they wouldn't be as judgmental as close relatives. Perhaps they would arrive at the home of a second cousin and claim to be married already. Or they could have been married in Jerusalem on the way to Bethlehem, only eight miles away. That might also explain why there was no room in the inn for Mary and Joseph. Even if Joseph wasn't that close to his relatives in Bethlehem, being unwed and pregnant was taboo. The young couple couldn't stay in Bethlehem with any family, so Jesus was born in a stable.

That's plausible, but why isn't it mentioned in the Bible? For one, pregnancy out of wedlock was just not spoken of as being possible in Jewish society, especially for respectable people. Even today it is looked down on by some. Also, the important part of the story isn't Mary and Joseph, it's that Jesus was born in Bethlehem. Nobody has disputed this assertion over the thousands of years of this story. People will point out the contradictions in Luke and Matthew, but they cannot pin down another birthplace for Jesus. With the preponderance of evidence about Jesus listed in historical sources, there is no doubt that he existed. In order to exist, he had to be born. He was born in Bethlehem, no matter the truth of how his birth happened.

Explaining Jesus' resurrection is also difficult. I have never heard of anyone being resurrected from the dead except in zombie movies. The fact that these movies are fiction can be used by doubters of Jesus that Jesus never existed. I will say that resurrecting someone from the dead is not beyond the realm of what is possible through God. Since I cannot prove the direct resurrection of Jesus, I will discuss why I believe it is possible that Jesus was resurrected. To start, there were no objections to Jesus' rising from the dead. A body was never found, just an empty tomb. If someone in the ancient world wanted to discredit Christians, it would be easy to do so by finding Jesus' body. There were also multiple witnesses to the handling of Jesus' body. Their testimony could contradict one another, but they don't.

To start, Jesus' body was claimed by Joseph of Arimathea. Joseph was a member of the Jewish Sanhedrin, according to Mark. As a member of one of the leading sects in the Jewish religion (the Pharisees, Sanhedrins, and Zealots were the three major divisions of Judaism at this time), Joseph would have access to the Romans in charge of the crucified bodies. The Romans and Jews would want the bodies removed from the crosses as fast as possible since Jesus was killed so close to the Passover, which would have begun at sundown the day of Jesus' death. There should not have been any objection when Joseph offered to take the body.

John writes that Joseph brought Jesus' body to a new tomb that had been built in a garden nearby. The idea being that the body would be placed in a tomb nearby and be out of the way for the Passover. It was just a temporary tomb and Jesus would be moved to a more permanent spot. Or at least that's how it appears. John also writes that Joseph had with him about seventy-five pounds of myrrh and aloe in order to wrap and treat the body. That is a ton of material to prepare a body for only temporary storage. So maybe it wasn't supposed to be a temporary tomb but actually a permanent one.

Also, after claims were made about Jesus being resurrected, why didn't Joseph come forward and claim that he was the one who took the body? He certainly would have been questioned by the Jewish authorities, who would hate to find out that the man they just killed was the Messiah sent from God. By having Joseph come forward and telling how he removed Jesus' body from the temporary tomb and placing it in another tomb, there might be no Christianity today. But he didn't do that.

Despite the massive amount of aloe and myrrh Joseph used, Mary Magdalene arrived at Jesus' tomb the day after the Passover. She was going to prepare the body properly as there probably wasn't a lot of time to do so before the sun set for the Passover. Typically, women were responsible for preparing bodies for burial. Then after one year, the tomb would have been opened and a woman would go in and collect the bones for storage in a box that would be placed in another tomb with bone boxes from other family members.

Mary Magdalene arrived at the tomb, she found the stone covering the entrance rolled away. Rolling away the stone and then taking the body away would have been difficult for her to do without someone seeing. If someone had seen a person roll away the stone or take the body away, then they would have certainly come forward and the Jewish authorities would have been glad to hear their story. Nobody did that. Mary Magdalene found the tomb empty with no explanation for why it was empty.

A further complication is that Jesus appeared after he was supposed to be dead. He appeared to Mary Magdalene at the tomb. She mistook him for the gardener. He appeared to two of his followers while they were traveling on the road away from Jerusalem. He appeared in Peter's home. He also appeared before his eleven disciples. He did this at least two times. The first time there were only ten disciples in the room – Thomas was elsewhere. When Thomas was told of what happened, he doubted that Jesus appeared. This is where we get the term "doubting Tom." Jesus later appeared before the eleven, with Thomas present. He encouraged Thomas to put his hands in his wounds to know that it really was Jesus come back from the dead.

Could all these people be hallucinating or lying? It is possible, but unlikely. Jesus appeared to different people in different places. Each of the appearances is similar though. Jesus just seems to appear out of thin air. Nobody is near Mary at the tomb and then there he is as the gardener. The disciples are in a locked room in Jerusalem and then Jesus appears. Two of his followers are walking along the road and then Jesus comes walking along the road with them. He also disappeared quickly. He left the disciples in the locked room. He left his two followers after sharing dinner with them. He left Mary at the tomb after telling her to go to his disciples and tell them that he is risen.

Only A Moral Teacher

Granted, believing in all this is probably difficult for you. You might be with me as to there being a historical Jesus, but all this Son of God stuff is bothering to you. Couldn't he just be a wise teacher? Unfortunately, he can't. Jesus did not just give valuable words of advice. He also spent a great deal of his preaching discussing God and the Kingdom of Heaven. There are some who will say that Jesus was an apocalyptic prophet who believed that the Kingdom of Heaven was going to arrive within his lifetime. Although there are passages where this interpretation can be made, it is difficult to reconcile this idea with the major point that Jesus predicted his own death and resurrection on at least three separate occasions. If Jesus really were an apocalyptic prophet then he would have acted like our modern doomsday fanatics – somehow looking forward to being alive at the end of the world. None of these modern doomsayers seem to believe that they will be back after three days. Most of these doomsayers are looked down upon by others in modern society because of their radical views. They are considered lunatics. But Jesus wasn't a lunatic. Or was he?

Jesus was killed because he called himself a king. He was talking about being the king of heaven because he was God. The local priests thought he was crazy for talking this way. They convinced Pilate that Jesus was claiming divinity and only the emperor could claim divinity. Therefore, Jesus was put to death for claiming to be divine. The crime that was written on a board placed on his cross called him "King of the Jews." Today if we hear somebody claim divinity, what is our reaction? We consider them lunatics as well. So was Jesus a lunatic? He can't be because he is also considered to be a wise teacher. So Jesus was not a lunatic as his teachings are considered sound and worthwhile even if his claims of divinity are a little crazy to some. The influence of Jesus' teachings reached into the twentieth century with such leaders as Gandhi, Martin Luther King Jr., and Nelson Mandela taking aspects of the words of Jesus in order to make their movements successful.

Then maybe Jesus was just lying about being divine. That would be safe. It preserves his reputation as a wise teacher and excuses all that Son of God stuff that is difficult to believe. But we still run into the same problem. Can a wise teacher also be a liar? I do not think so. Besides, was Jesus lying about his divinity? If he really did rise from the dead like he predicted, then he certainly wouldn't be a liar. He'd be the Lord.

British author and theologian C.S. Lewis presented the three L argument above. Jesus could either be a lunatic, liar, or Lord with the way he talked and acted. He could not have been anything else. Although this is only true if Jesus really existed. A fourth L has developed since Lewis' death. Jesus can also be a legend.

When I think of legends I think of King Arthur, Robin Hood, or Count Dracula. Each of them has some basis in history. Count Dracula is based on Vlad the Impaler. There were historical people named King Arthur and Robin of Locksley. So was Jesus a legend? There have been stories that have circulated about him for many, many years. Some of them are unbelievable. Could he rise from the dead? Did he raise others from the dead? What about making the blind see?

It is certainly possible that Jesus is just a legend. But his death is what doesn't sit right. Sure his crucifixion by Pilate could just be part of the historical Jesus, but why not put Jesus' qualities on someone else who didn't die by crucifixion? What I'm trying to say is that people like King Arthur, Robin Hood, and even Count Dracula are men of action. They are often violent. They're warriors as well as people who you can look up to, although maybe not in the case of Count Dracula. Still, none of their deaths are dealt with in a historical fashion like it is with Jesus. We are never told if Robin Hood dies. King Arthur doesn't seem to die either. Count Dracula does die, but he does so in such a way that it is clearly fiction. Vlad the Impaler was not struck through the heart by a wooden stake. Jesus' death is historically probable. It is not the stuff of legends.

Additionally, the Jews of the first century wanted a warrior who would overthrow Rome. They wanted to believe in a King Arthur or Robin Hood. Instead, they got a man who preached non-violence and talked about the Kingdom of Heaven. Once again Jesus does not measure up to our idea of a legend.

It would have been better if the teachings and resurrection of Jesus were combined with the great leadership of a warrior. A combination like Jesus of Nazareth, with his wise teaching and resurrection from the dead that symbolizes the ability of love to conquer death, and a great Jewish warrior like Judas Maccabee would have been the ideal if someone were to create a legend. This person could have fulfilled all the wants of Jews looking to believe in a Messiah. He would be a strong warrior capable of overthrowing Rome. He would be a wise teacher, well grounded in the teachings of God. That would be the ultimate Messiah a human could create. That does not describe Jesus. Therefore, Jesus cannot be a legend either.

The evidence for a historical Jesus is pretty overwhelming. It is up to you to decide what the historical Jesus was like. He was not just a wise teacher though. He also preached about the Kingdom of God and it would be untrue and unfair to characterize him as a wise teacher without mentioning God as the center of his teachings. So he was either a lunatic, liar, legend, or Lord. You have to choose one. Personally, I choose Lord. A lot of that has to do with the Gospels being eyewitness testimony, which is the subject of the next chapter.

5 THE GOSPELS AS EYEWITNESS TESTIMONY

The best source of information regarding the Gospels as eyewitness testimony is Richard Bauckham's book *Jesus and the Eyewitnesses: The Gospels as Eyewitness Testimony*. Bauckham goes into great detail about how the Gospels have all the hallmarks of being written by eyewitnesses and few of the characteristics of a work of fiction. I will briefly point out some of the general reasons why the Gospels were written by eyewitnesses and then I will look at some specific examples that show the eyewitness testimony.

The Bible is frequently used as a source of names. Christians have looked at the Old Testament and New Testament for names to call their children. Mary, John, Andrew, David, and Philip are all popular names that come from the Bible. In the first century, names were even more important. There were no last names. Either you were known in your cohort by your first name, or you were known by where you came from or who you were related to. We can look at the names of Jesus' twelve disciples for the use of first names, places, and relatives for names. By using a mixture of names in this way, the Gospels stand up as eyewitness testimony. It would be difficult for someone to make-up all the names of the disciples if there wasn't some truth behind the stories of Jesus.

For instance, all of the disciples except Judas Iscariot are from Galilee. Additionally, there was another Judas in the group. Previously I discussed how the name Judas was common among Jews in the first century. Also mentioned was the common practice of naming someone for where they came from if they were not locally known. So Judas becomes Judas Iscariot, which means Judas man of Kerioth. When Jesus left Nazareth, he became known as Jesus of Nazareth.

Now if your family was well known then you would be known through a relative. Jesus' disciples James and John were known as the Sons of Zebedee. Zebedee was a prominent businessman in the fishing industry.

He was so well-known that he knew the high priest in Jerusalem, which is why John and Peter are able to gain entrance into the high priest's courtyard on the night of Jesus' arrest. So Zebedee was well-known and if he was well-known, than his sons would take on his name when they interacted with people outside their normal cohort.

Interestingly enough, Jesus chose two sets of brothers to be among his twelve disciples. In addition to James and John, there were Simon and Andrew. Simon was renamed Peter, which means rock, by Jesus. Simon was a common name among first century Jews. Simon was also the name of another disciple in Jesus' group – Simon the Zealot. Simon the Zealot was known by this name because he was a member of the radical Zealot Jewish sect. They would eventually lead a revolt against Rome in 66 C.E. The result of this revolt was massive destruction in Jerusalem, including the destruction of the Jewish Temple. The Zealots were essentially urban terrorists. So Simon the Zealot would be aptly known and identifiable by this name. Returning to Simon and Andrew, Jesus renamed Simon as rock in order to get Simon to act more like a solid foundation in which Jesus could build the new Christian faith. Again, renaming someone like this would not occur if the work were fiction. Also, Simon's brother's name is Andrew. Andrew is a Greek name. There is no way that he was known as Andrew growing up. Most likely, he had a common Jewish name, like John or James or Jesus, just as his brother had a common Jewish name. Since there were already a great deal of common Jewish names in Jesus' group, Andrew would go by his Greek name for distinction. A similar belief is held for Philip, which is also a Greek name.

Not knowing why or how Andrew and Philip became known by their Greek names instead of their Hebrew names might open Christians up to claims that the Gospels are fiction. Wouldn't a fiction writer use a mixture of names from Greek and Hebrew in order to distinguish between characters? Not everyone could be named John or Simon, otherwise everybody would be confused. On the surface this seems like a legitimate objection. But upon closer examination it becomes clear that for some of the disciples, all we have is a name. Simon the Zealot for instance is only mentioned in the lists of Jesus' disciples. He says and does nothing throughout the rest of the Bible. Why even include him? Or why even make a distinction between him and Simon who is renamed Peter? If the names were being used to help characterize the fictional people then there might be a reason to use different names, but if they were their actual names then they should be allowed to keep them in the stories told about Jesus' life. There are two James in Jesus' group. One James doesn't do anything in the Gospels except have his name written in the list of disciples. The other is the brother of John and son of Zebedee. He is an active participant in the Gospel. He and his brother have their mother go to Jesus and request that they sit at Jesus' right and left sides in heaven. He and his brother also ask Jesus to call down fire on the Samaritans when they are inhospitable. If James is a distinct character in the Gospels, then why wasn't he given a Greek name like Philip or Andrew in order to distinguish him from the other James? The reason is because James was a real person. He was known as one of the sons of Zebedee. Therefore, James could not have a different name unless he had a nickname, which apparently he never had. The same goes for the other James. He is only mentioned in lists of the other disciples, therefore he is allowed to keep his given name.

One of the strongest cases for why the Gospels are true is this mixture of the Hebrew with the Greek. All of the existent manuscripts of the Gospels are written in Greek. Yet there are still Hebrew words preserved in the Greek. Therefore, either the people who wrote the stories down copied from Hebrew texts or the people telling the writers the stories spoke Hebrew. As mentioned in the last chapter, the word Messiah is Hebrew. It is included throughout the Gospels. The term Christ is only used in the later books of the New Testament when people like Paul, or Saul of Tarsus, write (Paul was known as Saul of Tarsus because he worked in Jerusalem but was originally from Tarsus on the Mediterranean Coast prior to being renamed Paul once he converted to Christianity) . This makes sense. Jews would be looking for a Messiah, the Hebrew term. Whereas a new convert to Christianity, and someone who did not grow up in the Promised Land, would not have any qualms about using the term Christ when describing Jesus.

Perhaps the most famous use of Hebrew in the Gospels is when Matthew records Jesus' final words as: "Eli, Eli, lama sabachthani." These Hebrew words are kept in the extant Gospel manuscripts. They are then translated into Greek (and eventually English) to give the meaning: "My God, My God, why have you forsaken me?" Although the theological question behind these words is intriguing, for this discussion it is important to note that the Hebrew is included along with a Greek, or in this case English, translation. If the Gospels were made-up by writers centuries later, like some skeptics believe, then why include Hebrew words? There probably weren't a lot of Hebrew speaking people in the Roman Empire when Christianity became the official religion in the fourth century. However, if Matthew spoke to someone who was at the cross that day, then they would have told him in Hebrew Jesus' final words.

A brief word about authorship is necessary right now. You might be wondering who the Gospel authors were, why they didn't use the first person like we expect when giving eyewitness testimony, and how we know their stories come from direct witness accounts. Now skeptics like to believe that the Gospels were written anonymously centuries after Jesus' death. This isn't the case. As expressed above, the use of Hebrew would have been eliminated if the Gospels were written centuries after Jesus' death. So skeptics only have the Gospels being written by Mr. Anonymous to go by. It is estimated that only about ten percent of the Roman Empire's population was literate. Therefore, a great deal of the religious teachings would have been done orally. The priests could read and write, but few others. With this in mind, let's look at the people credited with writing the Gospels.

The four Gospels are named after their authors. There are two books written by Jesus' disciples – Matthew and John. The other two are written by Mark and Luke. It is believed that Mark traveled extensively with Peter, the leader of the disciples, and Luke was a doctor who traveled with Paul, who became a convert to Christianity after being blinded for three days by the presence of Jesus. Paul is famous for the letters he wrote to early churches along the Mediterranean. He is also famous for being the apostle to the uncircumcised while Peter was the great apostle to God's People.

As further proof of authorship, each of these writers was probably educated. Matthew began his career as a Roman tax collector. He certainly would have needed to know how to read and write in order to do his job properly. He would also be familiar with languages other than Hebrew. Although it is unlikely that he wrote his Gospel in something other than Hebrew. Matthew's Gospel is specifically tailored to Jews. There are frequent references to the Old Testament in Matthew, which are not present in the other Gospels, including the above last words of Jesus, which refer to a prophecy from the Book of Isaiah.

John probably could also write. His father was a well-to-do businessman. John grew up privileged and was probably able to read and write because of his father's wealth. This doesn't mean that John lived in luxury all his life, but his father's success probably allowed him opportunities other disciples were unable to have. So why would John be able to write a Gospel and not his brother James? Well, James was the first disciple to die, not including Judas Iscariot. James was killed about a decade after Jesus' death. James' death is recounted by Luke in the Book of Acts, which examines the early church after Jesus' death and resurrection.

Scholars agree that the Book of Acts and the Gospel of Luke were written by the same person. Both books are addressed to the same person – Theophilus (believer). Theophilus is clearly a Greek name, so Luke had to be educated in Greek. Luke was a doctor. We know this because in the Book of Acts Luke tries to help a man who fell out a window while Paul spoke. So as a doctor, Luke had to be literate. With his close connection to Paul, one of the most important people in the early church, Luke would have great access to many eyewitnesses of Jesus' life.

Paul converted Luke to Christianity and in order to determine if Jesus really was the Son of God, Luke conducted an investigation. This investigation included interviewing eyewitnesses to Jesus' life. The results are the Gospel of Luke. Luke tells us as much in the first chapter of his book. He is attempting to put everything "in order as it happened." He has the investigative mind of a doctor. Also, as a doctor he would have been trained somewhere in the Mediterranean where he would have learned to write in the educated language of Greek. Unlike Matthew, Luke's book is specifically written for Gentiles since Paul was the apostle to the Gentiles and Luke was a recent convert to Christianity.

But there seems to be a big problem with Luke and the other Gospel writers not referring to themselves in the first person. This lack of first person in the Gospels is troubling to modern readers. We are so used to picking up a novel or non-fiction book and reading the word I. It just doesn't seem true to us that something can claim to be eyewitness testimony and yet the word I is nowhere to be found. John refers to himself as the disciple Jesus loved or Jesus' favorite disciple. This is the closest we get to a first person pronoun in the Gospels. To the Gospels credit, it was rare for a work of history to include the first person. Josephus uses the first person occasionally, but only when referring to a battle in which he actively participated. This is similar to the way John refers to himself as Jesus' favorite disciple. Additionally, the use of the author in third person was frequently used. The reason for this is that in works of history, the story is about the battle or person portrayed, not the author. How often do you hear about a "tell-all" book from someone associated with a famous person? The book is often about the person writing the book more than it is about the famous person. Since the Gospels were intended to be portraits of the life, work, and resurrection of Jesus, it would be inappropriate for the authors to make the stories about themselves. That does not mean that the authors don't include or take out certain stories.

John does not include the story about his mother going to ask to Jesus to see if her sons can sit sit next to Jesus in heaven. This story does not portray John in a good light, so he left it out. His cohorts however felt that it was important enough to include. John does make himself look good. Besides referring to himself as the disciple Jesus loved, John also includes the unnecessary detail that he is a faster runner than Peter. When the disciples learn that the tomb Jesus was buried in is empty, Peter and John run off to see. John states that he reached the tomb first and waited respectfully outside. Then Peter comes rushing up and enters the tomb without paying respect to the dead.

The story of Matthew's call by Jesus is longest in the Gospel of Matthew. Oddly enough, Matthew refers to himself as Levi in the text. Levi was his Hebrew name, while Matthew was his Greek name. As someone employed as a tax collector by the Romans, Matthew would have been able to write in the learned language of Greek. By referring to himself with his

Hebrew name, while he preferred to go by his Greek name, Matthew is able to distance himself from the first person pronouns that are so often present in the modern world. History in the ancient world rarely included the first person, even if the author was an eyewitness to an event described.

Luke does the best at staying out of his stories. He did not know Jesus directly, so he does not have to include himself in his Gospel. Since he was a frequent traveler with Paul and present at some of Paul's events recorded in the Book of Acts, Luke would have to make the occasional appearance. Luke does so with little fanfare. He refers to himself in the third person and gets out of there as soon as he can.

The oldest Gospel was written by Mark. Mark is regarded as Peter's translator. Peter most likely was illiterate. As the head of the church after Jesus' death, it would be incumbent upon Peter to travel around the Mediterranean to preach to Christians. He could only speak Hebrew, therefore he would need a translator when he traveled to areas in which Hebrew was not spoken. Enter Mark. He could translate for Peter and preserve Peter's memories of Jesus. He could also do all of this in Greek, since that was the language of the educated in the Mediterranean.

Another reason for Mark's Gospel being a collection of Peter's memories is that Peter is not made to look quite as bad as he is in the other gospels. Peter could be rash. For instance, in the famous story of Jesus walking on water, Peter got out of the boat in order to meet Jesus. Peter actually took a step onto the water, but then realized what he was doing and became scared. Jesus ended up having to save Peter. Rash decisions, like leaping out of a boat and attempting to walk on water, are what make Peter an enjoyable character in the Bible. If this were a work of fiction, then it would be expected that this rash man would frequently make rash decisions. This is the case in three of the Gospels. But it is missing in the Gospel of Mark. This has to do with the fact that Mark was relating Peter's memories. Of course we all look great in our own minds, so it is no surprise that Peter's rashness is diminished in the Gospel of Mark.

All the above is well and good, but what you really want is a title page with the author of the Gospel listed. Unfortunately that is not how ancient manuscripts were stylized. Ancient manuscripts were passed around through scrolls. The scrolls would be tagged, just like a piece of luggage, with the original author's name. In the case of the Gospels, the tags on the scrolls were Mark, Matthew, Luke, and John. Unfortunately, none of these tags have survived. So how do we know that Mark, Matthew, Luke, and John were originally tagged and are actually the authors of the Gospels? We have to turn to the eyewitnesses to the Gospels.

In the early second century, a man named Papias wrote about the Gospels and his experiences with meeting eyewitnesses to the life of Jesus. Papias wrote around the year 100 A.D., but none of his work survives.

What we have is quoted by early church writers. It is believed that Papias was the Bishop of Hierapolis, in what is now modern Turkey. As such, Papias was directly on the route between Rome and Jerusalem. He was in such a position that he would be able to meet and converse with people who knew the historical Jesus. It is said that he was friends with John, the author of the Gospel of John and the longest living of Jesus' disciples, as well as two of Philip's daughters.

Most importantly, what has survived from Papias' writings include his first-hand knowledge that the Gospels were written by eyewitnesses and that eyewitness testimony about the life and deeds of Jesus were being distributed around the Roman Empire. Papias makes it clear that he would consider anything less than a story by an eyewitness to be heresy. He vouches for the Gospels by stating that Mark was Peter's interpreter and that Mark wrote down "accurately as many things as he (Peter) recalled from memory" (Bauckham, 212). Therefore, it can be stated that Mark did not include a complete picture of Jesus' life. For instance, there is no birth story in the Gospel of Mark. The reason being that Peter was not present at Jesus' birth.

Regarding Matthew, Papias reports that the Gospel was written in Hebrew and that "each person interpreted them (the stories) as best he could" (Bauckham, 211). Again, Papias is not claiming that Matthew included a complete picture of Jesus, but that he was putting together Jesus' story the best he and those he knew could remember.

Nothing has survived regarding Papias' thoughts on the Gospel of Luke. Perhaps it could be said that Luke was not the actual author of the Gospel. Then again, there is the issue of the Book of Acts and Gospel of Luke being credited to the same author. It is just about universally agreed that the Book of Acts was written by Luke. Therefore, the Gospel of Luke should also be accredited to Luke.

Finally, Papias knew John. John was the longest living disciple. He lived out his later life alone on an island instead of being held in a Roman prison for being a Christian. John used his solitude to write. He wrote the Gospel of John and then later in his life he wrote the Book of Revelations. Now how did Papias know John if John lived in seclusion on an island? Well, John was an old man. He was not actively involved in the church, therefore he wasn't a huge threat to Rome. He was able to get away from the island every once in awhile. When he did so, he could have traveled through Hierapolis if he was making a trip to his original homeland.

Now you might be wondering how prevalent traveling over long distances was in the ancient world. Contrary to popular belief, people could travel long distances if they needed to or wanted to. For Jews living in Galilee, there was the yearly pilgrimage to Jerusalem. From Capernaum, a city in Galilee where Andrew, Peter, James, and John were from, the trip would be about 70 miles. Walking 70 miles to and from Jerusalem each year, not to mention the traveling Jesus and the disciples would do during the public ministry, would acquaint each man with the ability to travel great distances. Could an old man like John be able to make a long trip on foot from Greece to Israel? Possibly not. Another option is that Papias could have visited John. This could be more likely as the Romans might not object to an old man having the occasional visitor.

So in all, there is a case to be made regarding the Gospels as being authored by Mark, Matthew, Luke, and John. Certainly we would love to have a title page available in which it is undeniable that these four men were the authors. But much like the fact that Jesus never directly spoke the words "I am God," we can deduce from the evidence that there is a good chance the Gospels are really named after their authors. Let us now look at each Gospel in succession and how they exhibit hallmarks of eyewitness testimony. Tracking down the exact author of the Gospel is important, but it is even more important to the truth of Christianity if it can be proved that the Gospels contain eyewitness testimony.

The first book of the New Testament is the Gospel of Matthew. The book is attributed to one of Jesus' disciples, who would be a direct eyewitness to Jesus' teachings. This is present in the book, especially the testimony of Jesus' teaching and the discrepancy regarding Jesus' entrance into Jerusalem at the end of his life.

Jesus is perhaps most famous among non-Christians for his teaching. The majority of his most famous sayings are included in the Sermon on the Mount. The Sermon on the Mount is contained in its longest form in the Gospel of Matthew. Now it is not believed that the Sermon on the Mount was spoken in its entirety at one sitting. Rather, it is believed that the Sermon on the Mount is a collection of Jesus' greatest teachings. So it makes sense that Matthew would write the teachings in such a way.

He introduces the Sermon on the Mount by stating that Jesus taught on a mountain, Matthew does not specify which one, and that Jesus called his disciples around him. If Matthew, who was writing in Hebrew and contains a great deal of references to the Old Testament, were making this up, he would have specified the mountain Jesus stood on. For instance, the Mount of Olives outside of Jerusalem takes on great significance later in Jesus' life. Mount Sinai is the most famous mountain in the Old Testament. Yet, Matthew doesn't specify the mountain. This is because Matthew has just collected Jesus' teachings and ordered them in such a way that it appears that Jesus said these words at one time. The only time that we know Jesus is on a mountain is at the beginning when Matthew writes that Jesus called his disciples together and then started preaching the Beatitudes (the set of blessings Jesus gives to his audience that begin "Blest art…"). Once the Beatitudes are over, Matthew just records Jesus' teachings. He does not state that Jesus walked among the people gathered around him. It is just assumed by future generations that Jesus did this.

Now you might be angry at Matthew for implying that Jesus spoke the Sermon on the Mount once. You may even consider the way Matthew presented the teachings as a work of fiction. But Matthew uses a literary technique to cut down the time between Jesus' teachings. Matthew was with Jesus for nearly three years. Each and every one of those days Jesus taught to others. Some of what Jesus said was remembered, some was forgotten, sometimes Jesus repeated what he said over and over for new audiences. The Sermon on the Mount is a collection of the most important sayings from Jesus. They are presented as if Matthew was actually present when Jesus spoke. They are also presented as if Matthew had memorized the sayings after hearing them over and over. Matthew couldn't have remembered, in fact nobody could have remembered, the whole Sermon on the Mount if it only was stated once. Therefore, Matthew collected each of Jesus' most important teachings and put them in one part of his book. He might order the teachings under the heading of Sermon on the Mount, but that's just a literary technique. Future generations have fallen for Matthew's trick and believe the Sermon on the Mount was given at one time. It just isn't possible for people to remember Jesus' teachings if the Sermon on the Mount happened once. However, if Jesus frequently taught on mountains and used similar words when speaking, then it makes sense that Matthew would be able to recollect and order Jesus' sayings in one section of his Gospel. Matthew is practical when it comes to the teachings of Jesus. He isn't being a fiction writer. If he were, then there would have been a greater description of the reactions of the people on the mount or of the mountain itself.

Perhaps the greatest discrepancy in the New Testament occurs in the Gospel of Matthew. At the beginning of Jesus' last week of life, Jesus asked his disciples to go into Jerusalem and get him a donkey colt. This is done in order to fulfill a prophecy in the Old Testament in which the Messiah would come into Jerusalem on a colt. Now, the Gospel of Matthew tells the story a little different. Instead of the disciples taking just the colt, which is next to a donkey, Matthew writes that the disciples take a colt and a donkey. Presumably this means that on Palm Sunday Jesus entered Jerusalem riding both a donkey and colt. This is both difficult to do and plain ridiculous. So what happened? Did Matthew get it wrong? He is the one whose name is on the Gospel, therefore he takes the blame for getting it wrong.

However, Matthew's writing is famous for its relation back to the Old Testament. It is unlikely that he would mess up this reference to an Old Testament prophecy. He was attempting to reach Jews with his Gospel. A mistake like this would surely draw the ire of a great deal of Jews who knew the Old Testament backward and forward. It is my belief that Matthew got the prophecy correct in the original manuscript. It was some translator who made the mistake when the manuscript was copied. This makes sense as the people who would be copying the Gospel of Matthew would be those who were educated and familiar with the prophecy but might have a different interpretation of the prophecy. Either way, whether it is Matthew or someone latter who made the mistake, a mistake was made somewhere along the way. This is proof that the Gospels were written by human beings. God is perfect. Therefore, God cannot make a mistake like this. A human being is imperfect. Therefore, a human being can make a mistake like putting Jesus on both a colt and donkey.

The two examples from the Gospel of Matthew are intended to show that the writers of the Gospels were human beings. They made mistakes. They didn't include unnecessary details and even edited their accounts based on what was more efficient and effective for the reader. In this way, Matthew acts as a journalist. A journalist will attend an event that is three or four hours long. His story in the morning paper will only be a couple paragraphs long. He focuses all his attention on what was most important about the event. Matthew did the same thing with his Gospel. He included the most important teachings of Jesus in one spot under the heading of the Sermon on the Mount. Just because Matthew took some liberty with the way he arranged his stories and told them, doesn't mean that they aren't true.

The Gospel of Mark is the second book of the New Testament. Mark is also regarded as the oldest written Gospel. Peter features prominently in the book. This is also the only Gospel not to feature a Jesus origin story. It appears that Mark relies almost exclusively on Peter's testimony to complete this book. Peter is the most distinctive character among the disciples. He is the group's spokesman and usually the first to take action.

Two stories stand out as good examples of how Peter recollected some of Jesus' most famous tasks. First, there is the famous story of Jesus walking on water. In Mark Chapter 6 the story is recalled by Peter. He states that Jesus told the disciples to cross the Sea of Galilee on a boat and that Jesus would meet them on the other side in the morning so that they could teach. The disciples got into the boat while Jesus dismissed the crowd that gathered to hear him teach. Then Jesus went off to pray. During the night, the wind kicked up and the boat started to sway. The disciples awoke to see Jesus walking on the water toward them. Mark records that they were scared because "they thought he was a ghost." They cried out to Jesus in terror. It is clear that this reaction is believable and comes from someone who was actually there. Being afraid and thinking someone is a ghost is a natural reaction to seeing a man walk on water. Now if this were written by someone later who was trying to describe the glory of Jesus to make Christianity look good, then they would have left out the part of the disciples being terrified. Why would the disciples be terrified of the man who is supposed to be their savior? Shouldn't they be happy to see him in the midst of a storm?

Jesus then reassures the disciples. He tells them not to be afraid and then Jesus enters the boat. The winds immediately calm. Oddly enough, this story does not include the part where Peter sees Jesus and gets out of the boat to meet Jesus. The rest of the disciples might have been afraid, but Peter certainly wasn't. Instead, Peter was stupid. He rashly stuck his foot onto the water. Peter doesn't immediately sink. He only starts to sink when he realizes what he is doing. Jesus has to save him. So Peter accurately describes his feelings of fear and wonder while seeing Jesus walk across the water. Peter just fails to also mention that he acted like an idiot and jumped out of the boat to meet Jesus. It would be up to other Gospel writers to include this tidbit.

Perhaps the worst moment in Peter's life is when he denied knowing Jesus. He did this not once, not twice, but three times. Prior to Jesus' arrest Jesus warned Peter that Peter would deny knowing Jesus three times before the rooster crows. Peter said Jesus was wrong. Peter said that he would die before he denied Jesus. Yet, Peter ended up denying Jesus three times while Jesus was on trial before the high priest Caiaphas of Jerusalem. Through the connections of John, Peter was able to gain access to the courtyard outside of Caiaphas's house.

The first denial occurs when a servant girl of the high priest walks by Peter, who is near the fire. She says that Peter was with Jesus when Jesus was arrested. Peter denies this. He leaves the courtyard and stands in the entryway. The servant girl remarks to those standing around that Peter was with Jesus when Jesus was arrested. Once again, Peter denies this. After a little longer, those standing around say that Peter was a Galilean. Peter's accent would give him away. According to Mark, Peter "began to call down curses" and then denied knowing Jesus. The rooster crowed and then Mark writes that Peter "broke down and wept."

This story obviously makes Peter look weak and unfaithful. If it were not true then it would not have been included in the Gospel. What is the benefit to early Christians if the head of the Jerusalem church is exposed as a weak, faithless man during Jesus' time of need? There are also little details, such as a *servant girl* being the questioner, that have the hallmarks of eyewitness testimony. We remember odd little details like who asked us a question or who was around when we were going through an emotional time. Peter certainly could have remembered the details that have been preserved in the Gospels, but he might not have been able to remember exactly how tall the servant girl was or what she was wearing. These details are unimportant to the story being told however. It is the big picture details that matter.

The Gospel of Luke is a bit different from that of Matthew and Mark. Luke did not have a direct connection to Jesus. He became a Christian through Paul. So Luke had to go in search of eyewitnesses in order to figure out if the stories he heard about Jesus were true. His Gospel provides a bigger picture than that of Mark. He is also less concerned with writing for Jews, like Matthew. Luke states that his purpose is to investigate everything and put it down in an orderly fashion so people know about the life of Jesus. With this goal in mind, Luke was able to depend on more than just eyewitness accounts from disciples. He was able to speak to people who interacted with Jesus or who were present when Jesus spoke in public.

Prior to Jesus' public ministry, there was a man who drove the religious leaders of the day wild. This man, named John the Baptist, had a ministry at the Jordan River. He would preach about the need for everybody to repent their sins. Then he would submerge them in the Jordan River, upon which their sins would be symbolically washed away. Some of Jesus' disciples, such as Andrew and Philip, started out as disciples of John the Baptist. Jesus himself was even baptized by John the Baptist. John the Baptist's mouth got him into trouble however. He did not approve of Herod Antipas' new wife being a widow. Antipas was the ruler of Galilee following the death of Herod the Great. John the Baptist even called Antipas' new wife an adulterer in public. So Antipas had John arrested and thrown in the king's dungeon.

John still had followers though. Luke recounts how two of John's followers were sent to Jesus in order to ask if Jesus really was the Messiah. This story obviously comes from the two followers of John the Baptist. Luke tells how the two followers met with John the Baptist and how John wanted to know for sure that Jesus was the Messiah. Then the story follows the two men as they ask Jesus John's question. Jesus replies: "Go back and report to John what you have seen and heard: The blind receive sight, the lame walk, those who have leprosy are cleansed, the deaf hear, the dead are raised, and the good news is proclaimed to the poor." Essentially, Jesus is telling the followers to give their eyewitness testimony. He tells them to report back to John, who is in prison, that what they are seeing and hearing about Jesus is correct. Jesus is the Messiah.

Although this story is interesting, it does not serve much of a purpose from a Christian perspective. John the Baptist is most important to Christians because he is the one who first noticed Jesus as the Messiah. Why then would Christians want to keep a story about John the Baptist having doubts regarding Jesus? The only answer that makes sense is that the story is true. John the Baptist had doubts while in prison. He wanted to know directly from Jesus if Jesus was the Messiah. Jesus does not directly confirm this, but he does tell John's followers to testify regarding what they have witnessed and heard about Jesus. Luke includes this story in his

Gospel because it continues to complete the picture of Jesus, which is what Luke intended when he started writing.

Later in the Gospel, Jesus is teaching at the temple in Jerusalem. This annoys the religious leaders. They attempt to question Jesus as to his authority for saying and teaching the way he does. This story is not necessarily important, nor does it come from a disciple. Most likely, Luke's source is someone who was in the temple listening to Jesus preach. It could be a former Jewish priest who converted to Christianity or it could have been a Jew who converted to Christianity after hearing Jesus preach at the temple.

Luke records that the religious leaders came up to Jesus and asked: "Tell us by what authority you are doing these things. Who gave you this authority?" It is easy to read these words and tell that the religious leaders were looking for a conflict. They knew that their authority was being questioned by Jesus. No Jew in the first century could question a religious leader's authority without severe consequences. By asking their question, the religious leaders are trying to trick Jesus into saying something that will get him arrested. Instead, Jesus responds with a question. He asks the religious leaders if John the Baptist's ministry came from heaven or human origin. At this time, John was dead. Herod Antipas had him beheaded. Many of the people in the temple believed that John was a prophet and for the religious leaders to ignore a prophet was a blemish on them. So the religious leaders were put in a bad spot. They declined to answer Jesus' question because either way they would lose. If John's authority came from heaven then they would have been questioned as to why they didn't believe him. If they answered that John's authority was human origin then they risked starting a riot with John's supporters who saw him as a prophet, and who were also supporters of Jesus.

This is another interesting story, but really not one that is crucial for Christianity to sustain itself. The story just makes the religious leaders of the day look bad. Early Christians did not need to tell stories about religious leaders looking bad. Their belief in Jesus as the Son of God was enough to draw the religious leaders' ire. They did not have to drive the wedge between them and the religious establishment even further by retelling this story. Instead, Luke probably includes this story simply because it fills out the larger Jesus story. Between Palm Sunday and Good Friday, Jesus taught in the temple in Jerusalem. This story is just an example of what went on during the week Jesus taught. We don't even get an opportunity to hear what Jesus said that made the religious leaders question his authority. We get the second half of the story where Jesus makes the religious leaders look bad instead.

The preceding three Gospels are called the Canonical Gospels. They are the oldest of the Gospels. They are also the most similar. They contain many of the same stories. The Gospel of John is different. John wrote his Gospel after the other three were available. He most likely knew what was contained in the other three. John chooses to write a more spiritual Gospel. He is not concerned with an orderly picture of Jesus or a brief recount of his own memories of Jesus or trying to convince Jews that Jesus was the Messiah. John is only concerned with letting people know that Jesus is the Son of God. Jesus was a real human being who John walked with for three years, but Jesus also fulfilled all the prophecies expected of the Messiah. John's Gospel is the only one in which Jesus directly states that he is God and he has been sent by God the Father. Since John deviates a great deal from the other Gospels, and because in this one Jesus makes his most overt claims to divinity, skeptics and critics have dismissed John's work. They question its authenticity. They also debate if it was the work of an eyewitness.

Surprisingly, the Gospel of John does stand up well to the criticisms. It possesses hallmarks of being eyewitness testimony. Remember the discussion above about the race between John and Peter? This story is not necessary. It does nothing to further the story of Jesus' resurrection. Also, the Gospel of John is extremely accurate regarding first century Israel's geography. Many of the spots where Jesus preaches and heals are actually named. These places have been uncovered by archeologists. Unlike the Gospel of Matthew, where the Sermon on the Mount is just a mixture of sayings and the mountain is unnamed, the locations in the Gospel of John are important, so they are named.

One of those named locations is the Jordan River. The Jordan is the setting for one of the most powerful stories in John's Gospel. John recounts how Jesus called Andrew and Philip away from John the Baptist. Basically, John the Baptist looked at Jesus and said that Jesus was the Messiah. Andrew and Philip then turn and follow Jesus without asking him for permission or telling John the Baptist goodbye. This story certainly has the hallmarks of an eyewitness recollection. Andrew and Philip were both followers of John the Baptist. It makes sense that they would then follow the man who John points out as being the Messiah. Andrew gets his brother, Peter, to follow Jesus. Phillip does the same with his friend, Nathaniel. This is the only time in the Gospels where the story of Philip and Nathaniel becoming followers of Jesus is told. Someone as intimately connected to Philip and Nathaniel would know this story. John spent a great deal of time with the disciples and they would talk about how they came to follow Jesus. Since the Gospel of John came after the other Gospels, it makes sense that a new story like this would be included by someone who knew Philip and Nathaniel.

Again, this is an interesting story but not something that was necessary to help convince early Christians of the truth of Jesus' divinity. John the

Baptist was long dead prior to the spread of Christianity. Therefore, the opinion of John the Baptist that Jesus was the Messiah would not carry a great deal of weight with those on the fence about Christianity. Philip and Nathaniel were not major disciples of Jesus, but there were likely followers of the two who had heard the story of their conversion and would find the story interesting if included in a Gospel account of Jesus' life. What makes the Gospel of John so different from the others is the inclusion of stories like the above that we do not find anywhere else. Of course, since John considered himself to be Jesus' favorite disciple, we would expect some stories that feature inside information.

One such story occurs during the Last Supper. Hours before Jesus was arrested, he gathered his disciples together for the last time. He readily admitted to them that this would be the last time he would see them while he was alive. They didn't understand. He made his final preparations for them to take over preaching his word. As to be expected, John said that he had a privileged spot at the table. He was so close to Jesus that he was able to lay on Jesus' chest during the meal. He was also so close to Jesus that he was able to ask Jesus who was going to betray Jesus. Jesus replied that it would be the man who he served a piece of bread to next. Upon telling John this, Jesus served Judas a piece of bread. Judas took the bread and then left the Last Supper in order to make arrangements for Jesus' arrest.

Certainly there is room for doubt regarding this story. For one, none of the other Gospels report that anyone knew who was going to betray Jesus until it became clear it was Judas at the Garden of Gethsemane when Jesus was arrested. The other Gospels present the Last Supper as a time of confusion for the disciples. They do not understand the talk about Jesus leaving them soon. They are quick to deny that anyone would betray him. If John knew beforehand that Judas was going to betray Jesus, then why didn't he do anything to stop the arrest? In light of what would happen, namely that Jesus would be crucified and resurrected, John's not doing anything about Judas is not that big of a deal. Jesus was able to win despite Judas' betrayal. John could lean on Jesus' chest while Jesus told him who would be the betrayer and it wouldn't matter because Judas was not going to win. At the time though, it was very much in doubt. So either John was not given special knowledge from Jesus or he was because he was Jesus' favorite. But for whatever reason John decided not to act on the knowledge. Writing years later, John is justified in keeping silent because Jesus was resurrected.

Now John's story here could be true, but it needs to be met with a skeptical eye. The point of including this story, as well as any of the others mentioned, is to point out that eyewitness testimony is not perfect. There is not a one-size-fits-all criteria that can be applied. It is beyond the scope of this book to include an analysis of each of the stories in the Gospels, but it would be necessary to analyze each and every one to see if they pass the test of eyewitness testimony. You cannot simply claim that the Gospels were written centuries after Jesus died. That is not true. Nor can you claim that there are no mistakes in the Gospels because they are the divine word of God. Clearly there are mistakes. This is the case with eyewitness testimony. Think of eyewitnesses in court. There will be contradictions among what each person thought they saw. Suppose the case is about an auto accident. Everyone will agree that an accident took place. One person might have seen a white and a red car involved. Another, a silver and a red car. Someone might have seen a red truck instead of a red car. The eyewitnesses who composed the Gospels make similar mistakes. Did Jesus ride into Jerusalem on a colt and donkey or just the colt of a donkey? Did Jesus tell John that Judas was going to betray him or did John just add this later in order to make himself look like he was closer to Jesus than anyone else?

The stories chosen for analysis in this chapter are included because they contain elements of eyewitness testimony. For the most part though, the stories chosen are not the crux of the Gospels with the exception of the Sermon on the Mount. If John the Baptist sent people to ask if Jesus was the Messiah, what bearing would that have on early Christianity? The same is true about the conversion stories of Nathaniel and Philip. One of the criticisms of the Gospels is that they were fabricated to aid the growth of Christianity. Clearly moral teachings such as the Sermon on the Mount or the Passion and Resurrection of Jesus would be the most likely to be fabricated since they would have a huge impact on the beliefs of people. Yet there are more stories in each of the Gospels. These other stories are just as necessary in completing a portrait of Jesus. John the Baptist had doubts. Peter did deny Jesus three times. These stories are important because they are true.

So despite some of the contradictions and questions, overall the Gospels stand up under scrutiny. They have the hallmarks of being eyewitness testimony. With this being the case, and remembering that there is a great deal of evidence that the historical Jesus of Nazareth existed, then you've got to ask yourself: was Jesus really the Son of God? All it takes is a small leap of faith to answer yes.

6 MIRACLES

One of the biggest hurdles people have to believing in God is the existence of miracles. Miracles just seem too fantastic to be believed. How can the Red Sea be parted and one million people allowed to cross with no problems? Can a virgin really get pregnant? These are just two of the most famous miracles from the Bible. They are also two of the most important stories to the Jewish and Christian faiths respectively. They are proof, to those who believe, that God is at work in the world. But can they be believed?

As mentioned in Chapter 4 about the historical Jesus, when God is involved then anything is possible. Also, once Mary was impregnated, Jesus had to develop in her womb for nine months. He also came out of her as a baby and not a full-formed man. It is important to restate these parts of the story because it is easy to just assume that once one fantastical event occurs then all the rest are also fantastical. That is not the case. Once the Red Sea was parted and the Israelites exited safely, the Red Sea returned to its normal state.

Another important point that needs to be established about miracles is that by their very nature they are rare. They do not occur more than once. The Red Sea was parted one time in the thousands of years humans have recorded history. Jesus is the only human being believed to have been born of a virgin. When Jesus or Paul or Peter raised someone from the dead, it was only once. The most famous person to rise from the dead is Lazarus. He was Jesus' friend and Jesus brought him back to life after he'd died of a sickness. He did not bring Lazarus back multiple times. Lazarus would eventually die permanently, like all humans, but when he was brought back from the dead it was with no complications. He wasn't a zombie who preyed on brains or anything of that nature. The above stipulations, that miracles only briefly change what we consider the natural world and are one-time deals, needs to be remembered but those caveats still do nothing to make miracles more believable.

C.S. Lewis wrote an entire book about miracles, he even called the book *Miracles*, in which he went into great length about the world around us and how nature can be affected by miracles. His book is recommended if you really are curious about miracles and wish for a deeper philosophical probing. The above examples are his basic points about nature resuming after the miracle and miracles being rare. I will now divert from Lewis and examine the tenets of a miracle and how those tenets can be found in one of the rarest events of human history.

Arguments against miracles typically point out that because they are so rare, so unbelievable, and are tied to a divine being that can neither be seen or heard, then miracles are just too fantastic to be real. In short, miracles are so unpredictable that they cannot be legitimately considered a part of nature. They cannot be studied by scientists because there is such a small sample size. It is a lot easier to predict the weather than miracles. Although some might disagree that the weather can be predicted, especially if the weatherman said there would be no rain and you end up getting drenched on your way to work. Still, we have developed models and knowledge of weather patterns so that we can predict the weather down to the hour. The weatherman might not always be correct, but he is a lot more accurate than you would be if you tried to predict the next time the Red Sea will be parted. Even the Israelites wouldn't have believed the Red Sea was going to be parted. Their first reaction was probably that there would be a fleet of boats or even a giant ark like Noah had to ferry them across the Red Sea. When there was no sign of a boat their next reaction might have been that someone played a trick on them. They escaped the Egyptians to reach the beach of the Red Sea only to have it act as a natural barrier against them. They might have even panicked because slaughter by the Egyptian army seemed imminent. Instead, God parted the Red Sea and the Israelites became free.

The unpredictability of the event is what makes it seem so much like fiction. If someone were writing a fictional story about the Israelites leaving Egypt, they might write that the Red Sea parted, but someone who is actually in the situation would never believe that was possible. Their thoughts would be on what they experienced. Nobody had ever experienced or even heard of the possibility of the Red Sea parting before. To make matters even worse, some unseen divine being was the cause of this miracle. So when you add-in the divine nature of miracles you really have something out of fiction.

There are non-miracles that seem too unreal to be true, except that they are real because there is documentation. Take for instance The Holocaust. The Holocaust is used here, not because it is a miracle, but in order to show that unfathomable, well-documented events can occur and people can still choose not to believe in the reality of these events. One of the biggest objections to miracles is that they are too unbelievable, too fantastic to believe. Yet they were well documented for their times. With no video or photographs available, it was up to written and oral accounts of events to spread around an area as news. Those who lived in the Promised Land knew that the Israelites came out of Egypt and they did so because the Red Sea parted. Some surrendered to them because they heard and believed this event to be true. With the Holocaust, there is more concrete evidence, yet the event is no less unbelievable.

As early as 1925, writing in *Mien Kompf*, Adolf Hitler espoused his raciest and anti-Semitic remarks regarding those of the Jewish religion and essentially anybody who was not part of the Arian race. The ideal Arian possessed blonde hair and blue eyes. Hitler had neither. Although rationality never works with people like Hitler. Still, he was given a prominent place in the Nazi Party. Through his raw emotion and oratory skills he was able to convince the German people that their poverty was caused by foreign powers and Jews internally. If the Jews were eliminated, then the Germans would become prosperous again. The desperate people allowed this man to gain more and more power because he brought the working German prosperity like he promised. By 1933, Hitler became dictator of Germany.

As dictator, Hitler was able to meld his racist ideas with official German policy. Soon, Jews lost their businesses, their rights, and their citizenship. They were second class citizens in Germany. They stood out by having the Star of David sown on their clothing. Germans were encouraged to blame the Jews for all of Germany's problems. They were also encouraged to take their abuse of the Jews from the verbal into the physical. Authorities looked the other way or helped physically abuse Jews. There was the Kristallnacht in November 1938. At least 91 Jews were killed in a night-long attack by Germans in Jewish neighborhoods throughout Germany and Austria.

The rest of the world watched and didn't do anything to save the Jews except give Hitler the occasional verbal reprimand. Racist comments and even physical violence against another race of people have been common throughout human history. Therefore, the persecution of the Jews at this time does not have the unbelievable quality of a miracle. Hitler told everyone that he would blame the Jews for Germany's problems when he wrote *Mien Kompf*. He was just putting action to his thoughts. What happened once Germany invaded Poland is where the miraculous qualities come into play.

Once the Germans conquered Poland, Hitler had a problem. Sure France and England declared war on Germany, but there was a more pressing issue. Poland had a huge population of Jews. They needed to be moved in order for more land to be available for the superior Arian race. Hitler decided to get rid of the Polish Jews by resorting to violence. German troops were required to shoot Polish Jews after the Jews were forced to dig trenches in the Polish countryside that would act as mass graves. This was an efficient way to deal with the "Jewish problem." The only drawback to Hitler was that his master race had feelings. It was brutal for the troops to gun down innocent people day after day and then bury them in mass graves. Morale among the German S.S. troops who did most of the killing was low. A new way of getting rid of the Jews would have to be found. Unfortunately, this part of our story is also devoid of miraculous qualities. Mass genocide of a group of people is not new among human beings. It didn't even end with World War II. There has been mass genocide perpetrated in African Civil Wars, especially in the Congo, that is still going on in the twenty-first century. In the late-twentieth century, Slobodan Milosevic led a mass genocide policy in Kosovo.

The Final Solution to Hitler's "Jewish problem" came when concentration camps were turned into death camps and smaller, death specific camps were established. Now a concentration camp was not new. At the same time as Jews, gypsies and other undesirables in the Nazi empire were being shipped to concentration camps in order to make room for the Arian race, President Franklin D. Roosevelt issued an executive order that moved those of Japanese descent into camps located in the interior of the United States. The German concentration camps were much more brutal than those of the United States, but the concept was similar. Fear of a different race caused these leaders to move masses of people away from their homes. Hitler took it one step further though. He demanded that the concentration camps now focus on killing Jews and not on exploiting the Jews as a cheap workforce.

The Allies knew about the concentration camps. They knew that Jews were forcibly being removed from their homes and being shipped to these camps. Occasionally there would be a story in the newspaper or a magazine that reported the atrocities that occurred at these camps. By and large though, it wasn't until the Allies made a push into Germany and came upon these camps that their reality reached the West. Videos were taken of the deplorable conditions. *Life* magazine ran a huge pictorial about the camps. Survivors started to tell their stories. The Allies were horrified by what happened. It was unbelievable that a nation that was supposed to be so civilized and advanced, like Germany, would be capable of undertaking such a massive genocide.

Hitler told the world that he hated the Jews. The world listened and dismissed him. They knew about the abuses. They knew about the massive movement of people. Killing six million people deliberately and systematically like the Nazis did though was unbelievable. Using gas chambers and crematories to dispose of bodies was unbelievable. Developing an efficient killing factory at Treblinka was beyond the realm of possibility to the human beings living in civilized countries. This unbelievable aspect is what causes the Holocaust to have miraculous qualities, although certainly not a miracle. Like a virgin getting pregnant or the Red Sea being parted, the world could not fathom such a massive amount of killing done in such a way.

The unbelievable quality still reverberates today in the form of Holocaust deniers. Despite the videos, pictures, stories, and structures that remain, some do not believe that the Holocaust occurred. It is just too gruesome to believe that a group of people would be eliminated in such a way. Of course, there is some Anti-Semitism in their denials, but how is that different from those who aren't religious denying the parting of the Red Sea or the birth of Jesus from a virgin? Atheists, who are anti-religious, will be the ones who deny the believability of the Biblical miracles, just like the Anti-Semite will do the same with the Holocaust.

With the above in mind, it can be said that if there is one quality that ties all miracles together it is faith. Moses had faith that God would save the Israelites, therefore the Red Sea was parted. Mary had faith that God was asking her to carry the Messiah, therefore she was able to become pregnant despite being a virgin. The tie between faith and miracles is best expressed in the story of Jesus walking on water. His disciples awoke in the night to see Jesus walking on the Sea of Galilee toward their boat. Peter, Jesus' lead disciple, got out of the boat and actually took a few steps on the water. When he realized that he wasn't supposed to be walking on water because he was a human being, he started to sink. Jesus saved him. Then Jesus admonished him from not having enough faith. When Peter had faith he was able to walk on the water just like Jesus. When he started to lose faith, when he saw that his actions were contrary to his expectations and beliefs about what a human being can and cannot do, he started to sink.

Also, at different times, Peter and Paul brought people back from the dead. In one story, a man fell out of a window while Paul preached. A crowd gathered around the fallen man and it was clear that he was dead. Paul was unsure of what to do. He basically fell over the man and asked God for help in healing him. Through Paul, God brought the man back to life. This man would go on to live a regular life, again no zombies here, but he owed his life to a miracle. Paul didn't have medical training. He had faith and he used that to bring the man back from the dead.

Does this mean that someone has to have a lot of faith in order for a miracle to occur? If they don't have enough of this unquantifiable amount of faith will a miracle never occur even though they pray for one? I can't answer either of those questions. I just want to point out that the miracles listed in the Bible are basically all faith based. God performed these miracles in aid of people who had great faith in Him for at least a short amount of time. Perhaps the best example of this type of miracle is when David fought Goliath.

Little David took on mighty Goliath with just a sling-shot and stone. David knew beforehand that God promised him the kingship of Israel. He had faith that God would deliver on His promise. Therefore, he was not worried about facing a bigger and stronger opponent. David had faith in God. Faith gave David confidence.

The trust that David had led to his being able to beat Goliath even if the chances of him doing so were low. However, the chance David had would be higher than that of the Red Sea parting. It is not completely unheard of in human history that a stone is able to knock down a great beast. The cavemen resorted to stones and small spears to kill large animals like Great Elks and Woolly Mammoths. So when David took up the sling-shot and stone, his fellow Israelites could at least believe in the possibility of the tactic working even if the odds of it doing so were small.

The point of the David and Goliath discussion is that although miracles may look impossible on the surface, they are quite grounded in the natural world that we know and understand. This is especially true of miracles originating with humans, such as David against Goliath. The chances of something like David's sling-shot being able to take down Goliath is so statistically small that it can be considered to have miraculous qualities. This small statistical chance is why we refer to events in everyday life as miracles. Take the Miracle on Ice for instance.

A group of young American college players squared off against the most powerful hockey team in the world, from the U.S.S.R., in the 1980 Winter Olympics in Lake Placid, New York. This was only the semifinal match, but it had a lot more riding on it than the gold medal game. The game took place during the heated Cold War. There were the hated Ruskies going up against the hardworking Americans. The game was played on American home ice. Despite the home ice advantage, there was no way the experts were going to pick against the powerful U.S.S.R. They had all the talented players. They were the world's dominant hockey power. They were expected to win. They were going to win. Yet they lost.

The Russians didn't just lose. They lost in heartbreaking fashion. If the Americans had come out and just dominated play from start to finish then the win would have been shocking, but not called the Miracle on Ice. In order for the game to be referred to as a "miracle," the game had to be close, intense, and the Americans had to be losing late. The game had all of these. It looked hopeless for the Americans. It looked hopeless for the Israelites when they reached the Red Sea. It looked hopeless for the man who fell out of the window during Paul's preaching. It looked hopeless for David when he stood opposite Goliath with only a sling-shot. Then the miracle happened. The Americans scored a late goal to take the lead. The Red Sea parted. Paul brought the young man back to life. David's stone knocked out Goliath. Then there was great rejoicing. It seemed like the whole country rallied around the American hockey team. There were celebrations across the United States. It was more than a hockey game. It was a triumph of capitalism over communism. There was great celebration by the Israelites when they reached the Sinai Peninsula. This was a triumph out of slavery. Paul triumphed over death. David triumphed over tyranny. These miraculous accomplishments were celebrated and talked and discussed for many years to come. You remember where you were when you watched the United States score that winning goal against the U.S.S.R.

So the Miracle on Ice does share some qualities with the Biblical miracles, but there are major differences. For one, there is the probability of events. It was conceivable that the United States would win the game. The probability wasn't high, but it was not out of the realm of possibility that the United States would win. When the Israelites stood at the shore of the Red Sea, as mentioned above, there was little belief that the waters would part for their crossing. Also, there is the divine nature of the miracles. Even the most ardent patriot would have a tough time convincing somebody that God wanted the United States to win a hockey game. God is pleased with all his creations. He delights when they delight. But in sports, there has to be a winner and a loser. God does not take glee when a team loses. Finally, there is the fact that the Miracle on Ice is well documented. The game was broadcast live to a worldwide audience. Highlights have been shown in the years following the game. Newspaper reports and photographs depict the events of the game. Then there are the players and coaches and fans who experienced the game firsthand. After the game they could recall their observations and thoughts of what happened. Eyewitness accounts are all that are available from the Biblical miracles. The man who experienced being resurrected from the dead by Paul would certainly remember being saved, as would those who were at the event, including the writer of the story – Luke. But photographic and video evidence were not available in Biblical times. It is difficult for a modern audience to take these stories as being real because of this lack of physical evidence.

Fortunately miracles do not occur every day. The likelihood that you or me will ever see or experience a miracle is rare. This is a good thing. If a miracle occurs then it means that you are in such a bad situation that the only way to get out of it is through a miracle. You are a slave in Egypt and the only way to break the bonds of slavery is for the Red Sea to part. You die by falling out of a window and the only way to bring you back is for a man to lay on you. You are in need of a Messiah to overthrow Roman oppression, so a virgin is picked to conceive the Chosen One.

To distill the miracle discussion; although rare, they do happen. They are by definition unbelievable. They occur and disrupt nature, but nature returns to its regularly scheduled program. The miracle is typically tied in with those who have great faith. Finally, in order to be considered a true miracle, and not something that is given the term of miracle, like the Miracle on Ice, a divine quality must be present. God has to intervene on behalf of the faithful to save them from something, whether slavery, death, or oppression. Now, if God rewards the faithful with a miracle when they need Him then there has to be a way to contact Him. This is done through prayer, which is the subject of the next chapter.

7 PRAYER

Prayer is common to just about every religion. It seems simple. It's supposed to be a conversation between you and God. Yet it can also be complex. How do you talk to God? How do you strike the balance between selfishness and thankfulness? If you are silently praying in a group, how long do you take to pray? More importantly, you want to know if prayer works. Will God give me everything I ask for? No. Will God miraculously heal a child with cancer if I pray hard enough? I can't answer that, but nothing you pray for is ever guaranteed to come true. That is why prayer is so difficult.

It is common for Christians to take time to talk to God and ask for things, but He doesn't always deliver what we want. Instead, He gives us what we need, even if we don't think we need it at this particular time. Think failure. We don't want it, yet sometimes we fail at what we do. Each time you fall, you have the opportunity to get up or give up. Through God, you are able to get back up and become a stronger person after you've fallen. Praying to God for guidance in times of struggle or failure can help get through the difficult time.

At its most basic, prayer is simply a personal conversation between you and God. This can be done in the confines of your own home, while you're sitting in church, in a small group of people, or in a congregation full of thousands. Why do you need to have a personal conversation with God? Isn't God an all-seeing, all-knowing being? Can't He read your thoughts? If He can, then there should be no reason for prayer. God knows your wants and desires. He can see how hard you work trying to pay the bills, juggle a career, and manage a family. Maybe all you need is for that holiday bonus to be just a bit larger this year so you can get a new car for the family. Do you need to pray for this or shouldn't the all-seeing, all-knowing God be able to tell that you want something?

Unlike people, God is a mind-reader. Jesus is frequently depicted as being able to read the minds of the people around him. He does this with the Pharisees, the leading priests of the day, when they wish to question his reasoning of a problem but are too afraid to come out and ask him. Jesus just answers their thought questions. He also does this with his disciples when they are too afraid to ask him questions when his teaching gets too difficult for them to understand or believe. Since Jesus is the Son of God, being one with the Father, and he is able to read people's minds, then that means that God is also able to read a person's mind. So if God can read your mind, then why pray? Also, you might be a little uneasy now that you know God can read your thoughts? God judging you for your actions is one thing, but what about him judging you for your thoughts. When someone cuts you off in traffic, you get angry. Maybe you even think what you'd like to do to them at the next stoplight. Or perhaps you think bad thoughts about what can happen to their car, like suddenly their tire blows out and they go careening into the guardrail. This is just a momentary thought that helps give you control and satisfaction of the situation. It isn't something that you would ever seriously hope for or consider doing. Does God know that though? Of course He does. It is true that God can read your thoughts, but it is also true that He is just and righteous and will not hold a momentary thought against you. Especially when this thought is designed to give you comfort in what can be a frustrating situation.

So now that you are comforted that God will forgive you for your temporary and emotional thoughts, why exactly do we still need to pray? Well, prayer is an opportunity for you to remove all of the clutter from your mind and focus all your attention on God by turning your thoughts to God.

So what should you talk about when you talk to God? The most popular prayer is the personal prayer to God in hopes that He will fulfill a wish. It may be for a promotion, a new car, a girl to accept your invitation to go out together, or any other want that you have. Unfortunately, this type of prayer gets you in trouble. God is not a wishing well or slot machine. You cannot ask, ask, ask and always get, get, get without putting in work or helping yourself. God provides. You must make the most of what He has provided for you.

The most popular form of prayer while in a group is the prayer of thanks. This is commonly seen right before a group of Christians eat a meal. They give thanks to God for providing them with food, drink, and fellowship. They also ask that God continue to watch over them and continue to let them have good health. The prayer of thanks is also popular in a congregation. The pastor will typically give thanks to God for allowing everyone to be together and for His presence to come over those in the congregation. Then the pastor will ask that He continue to watch over the congregation throughout the rest of the week. These are the most basic forms of the prayer of thanks. This prayer of thanks should be included in your personal prayers as well.

It is important to include the prayer of thanks in personal prayers because if you only ask for things in your prayers then you are bound to be disappointed. God is not Santa Claus. It would be easier to believe in Him if He were like Santa Claus. After all, the most popular time for people to attend church is Christmas Eve. Maybe more would go to church throughout the year if they felt that God were like Santa Claus and could give them whatever they wanted. But then life wouldn't be fun. It would boring if everything you wanted in life was just given to you. Part of the joy of achieving a goal is the struggle you go through to accomplish that goal. The difficulties you went through to get what you wanted help develop who you are as a person. God knows that it is in your best interest for you not to get everything you want.

God also doesn't make bargains. We've probably all made this prayer to God when we were young children. We've asked God for something. Typically it is insignificant, but it really matters to us at the time. It could be something like a parent being able to take you to the store so that you can get a toy. Or better yet, that the toy can be yours as a Christmas or birthday present. You make a bargain with God. You tell Him that in return for your getting the toy, you will do something for Him. This is also insignificant, but is really hard for you. Maybe you won't complain every evening when you have to take out the trash or wash the dishes. Or maybe you tell God that you're going to be nicer to your sister. Either way, you make a deal with God. You get something and He gets something. But just to make sure that you don't get the short end of the deal, you cross your fingers or don't close your eyes. This way, if God does not keep up His end of the bargain then you don't either. You have an out. You also have an out if God does keep His end of the bargain. If you get that toy then you tell God that the bargain does not count because you crossed your fingers or that you didn't close your eyes. You've pulled one over on God. At least that's what you think. You can't bargain with God because it isn't your world – it's God's.

Luckily we grow and develop and do not play the bargaining game with God. At least, we don't do it quite as overtly. We understand that we are not perfect people. Maybe you're having trouble with your spouse or another family member. You tell God that you're working on improving this relationship and that you'll continue to work at improving the relationship. But what you'd really like is for God to do something for you. That's the real reason why you are praying. God does not bargain though. You can ask and you can bargain, but it does not matter to God. He does what is best for you, according to Him.

Since God really is all-seeing and all-knowing, that means that He knows the future. He knows what is going to happen to you before you do. Since God has this knowledge, then why pray? This is an idea that I struggled with greatly. Having a one-sided conversation with someone I was pretty sure existed, but was not completely convinced, was difficult enough. Knowing that God also knew the future made prayer even more difficult. He could see my thoughts, so He knew my desires. He knows my future before I do, so why should I pray if everything is essentially pre-determined?

There are two reasons to continue to pray even if you think everything is already pre-determined by God. First, you do not know the future. God is the only one who knows the future. Since you do not know the future then it is better to be safe than sorry. Some people become Christians for the sole purpose that they do not want to spend eternity in hell. They aren't completely convinced that there is a God, but they want to be safe for eternity. Since they do not know for sure what happens when they die, they choose to become Christians. The same reasoning can be used as a reason to pray.

Secondly, the prayer is already built in. That is to say that since God knows the future, so He knows when you are going to pray to Him. The prayer is built into your future. This is not an easy concept to explain, but it makes sense. Since God knows the future, he also knows that you are going to pray to Him and ask for something. The forthcoming prayer factors into the ultimate end that God decides. Essentially this is just a variation on the first reason. You do not know, but God knows. God knows that you are going to pray and that can influence the future event because it occurs before the future event. Since you do not know what is going to happen, it is best to pray.

If you aren't completely confused right now, I want to give you a few examples of the power of prayer. After Moses led the Israelites out of slavery in Egypt, God asked him to spend forty days on Mount Sinai. Moses did as he was told. He placed his brother, Aaron, in charge of the Israelites while he was gone. Moses received the Ten Commandments while away. Aaron did not do a great job of leading the people. The people created a Golden Calf and made sacrifices to it. They believed this Golden Calf, and not God, was the reason why they were able to escape Egyptian slavery. Moses came back to the Israelites and saw what they were doing. He was so mad that he threw down the stone tablets containing the Ten Commandments. God was also displeased. He was so displeased that He was going to destroy the Israelites. Moses begged God not to do it. He fought for the Israelites and God relented. God did not kill the Israelites, but let them live. Now you probably aren't going to be able to make a direct appeal to God in His presence like Moses, but you can make a direct appeal to Him through prayer. Moses essentially prayed to God that He spare the Israelites' lives. God listened and allowed them to live. Of course He knew that He wouldn't kill the Israelites. He also knew that Moses would beg for their lives. Moses did not know any of this. Moses made his appeal to God and God granted his prayer.

Jewish history is filled with similar stories as the above. In fact, the whole Old Testament can be summed up as God telling the Israelites that they will be His people and He will be their God. Yet the Israelites do not live up to their end of this bargain. It is the only bargain God made throughout the Old Testament. All the Israelites had to do is be faithful to Him. They aren't. They stumble and fall as humans do. Yet He always takes them back because He is full of grace and love. When the Israelites find themselves on their own and their lives are miserable, they turn back to God. They offer up prayers and He answers them. No matter how many generations slip and fall when it comes to faithfulness, God forgives and helps. He is there to answer their prayers. He just might not do it immediately or in the way we wish.

Not having your prayers answered the way you wish is probably the most frustrating part of being a Christian. You are supposed to be a believer in God. You should get some reward for that belief. Shouldn't that be the answer to your prayers? But that is not how God works. We have doubts and fears and sometimes use prayer to ask God for advice or guidance. When our prayers aren't answered to our satisfaction, we feel like God wasn't listening. But everyone has doubts and fears and doesn't have all their prayers answered. Even Jesus had doubts and fears. Prior to his being arrested in the Garden of Gethsemane, he spent the evening in prayer. Not all of what Jesus said has been preserved, but the gist is that he was afraid and did not want to be arrested and crucified. Eventually he came to the conclusion that it was God's will that he would die via crucifixion. Once he accepted his fate, he asked God for the strength to go through with the whole ordeal. So the world might not be the way we wish, but it is important to continue to pray. God hears the prayers and they are built into what happens to us in the future. If you need further reasons to pray, then look at Jesus. Even he prayed. If the Son of God prayed, then you should pray as well.

If it's important to pray, then how should you pray? In the Book of Matthew, The Lord's Prayer is given as an example, spoken by Jesus, of how we should pray. It is the famous prayer that begins with "Our Father, who art in heaven." You are probably familiar with this prayer if you grew up going to church or even if you just wander in every Christmas or Easter. It is a tried and true standard that seemingly everyone in the congregation knows. If you are looking for a way to start a conversation with God, begin with the Lord's Prayer and then add in your own thoughts.

There is the running conversation type of prayer. Since God is all-knowing and all-seeing, then He knows all your thoughts. You can turn your attention to God when you are taking a walk in the morning or doing some other outdoor activity that isn't too stressful on the mind. Instead of day-dreaming, turn your thoughts toward God. You don't even have to formally address God during the running conversation prayer. You can just think. You can think about God. You can thank Him for the natural beauty that you are walking through. You can ask Him for help with a problem that you are having in your life. You can address many topics when you employ the running conversation prayer. The most important aspect, what makes it a prayer, is that you are addressing God in some way. You make a specific effort to think of God when you start the running conversation prayer. That way your prayer is separated from what would normally be just a day-dream. God can see your day-dreams, but you can't expect Him to act on the day-dream unless you directly think about Him and ask Him for help.

There is also the personal, private prayer that you do in your home. How do you address God in this type of prayer? What do you think of? Some people say that they picture Jesus in their mind and then address their silent prayer to this image. If this technique works for you, then that's great. It is a lot easier to put a face on an all-knowing, all-seeing God. Otherwise, you just have a face in the clouds, like the images we have of Zeus or some other Greek god. It is difficult to picture God's immensity. Focusing on Jesus is a lot easier. Although there is one issue with having a picture of Jesus in your mind – we do not know what Jesus looked like. He never posed for a sculptor in the first century and we did not have photography, video, or portrait painting to give us an image of him. What we consider to be the image of Jesus is something the Europeans came up with during the Renaissance. This picture of Jesus works for the purpose of focusing a prayer, but just understand that the image of Jesus you have in your mind might not be what the historical Jesus actually looked like.

If focusing on an image of Jesus is too difficult or weird or for some other reason you are unable to do it, then my suggestion is to do your best to clear your head. Think of heaven. We think of heaven as a lot of white light and clouds and cleanliness. Think of the white light when praying. This will clear your mind and allow you to focus on directing your prayer to God. Ultimately though, prayer is a personal conversation between you and God. Think about whatever you want so long as you are able to focus on God.

The most difficult type of prayer to sit through might be the group prayer. It is a common prayer. It can be done prior to eating a meal, while in church, prior to communion, or as a group when you pray for someone.

If you are praying for someone, you should have a picture of them in your mind. For the other examples of group prayer you might not have an easy object to picture in your mind. It would be nice if you could think about Jesus or the image of heaven, but it is not always that easy. You thoughts might be on the juicy food in front of you. You may not want to be in church at the moment of prayer and want to spend the time day-dreaming or even resting for a few minutes. Or you might not care for what the person praying has to say. How do you focus on God in these situations? I have found that focusing on the words is the best practice. You might not like what the person is saying, but there will be something that you agree with. When you find that part of the prayer that you agree with, then let those words linger in your mind until the person says something else that you agree with. By focusing on the words that are spoken, you are clearing your mind for God and you are adding your thoughts to the prayer that is being said. The point of the group prayer is for the group as a whole to ask God for guidance or for the group as a whole to give thanks to God. If you are not focusing on the words of the prayer, then you are not being a full participant in the group. Therefore, the point of praying as a group is lost.

Finally there is the private/group prayer. This is typically done prior to the taking of communion. Each person is given an opportunity to pray for forgiveness prior to the group taking communion. Obviously you should be focused on Jesus or heaven or whatever image works for you when you ask for forgiveness. You should continue to pray until you have confessed all your sins since the last time you took communion. The purpose of the prayer before communion is to ask forgiveness. Use this opportunity to your advantage by asking for forgiveness of your sins. But if you are like most people, then after the first three or four sins, you start to feel uneasy. It can be a long list of sins. Typically I refer to the fact that I know that I've sinned a lot and that God knows that I've sinned a lot. I don't have the hours of time that it would take to count all my sins. After three or four major sins that I have on the top of my head, I let God know that I know about the other sins. I tend to open my eyes around this time to see where everyone else is at. If everyone else is still praying then I move on to a prayer of thanks. I give my prayer of thanks, open my eyes and check around. I then go to a prayer for people that I know who are struggling and need help. I open my eyes after each prayer and typically there will be a few others in the group who have their eyes open. Each time I open my eyes, I reset the palette so to speak. God has received my last prayer. Now I can focus my thoughts on the new prayer.

Prayer is a tool used by Christians to have a direct and personal conversation with God. It can be done privately or in groups. This chapter has been designed to give examples of how prayer is conducted and how it works. Prayer does not always work though. Sometimes prayers fail. We question why God does not answer our prayers. Are we not believers? Doesn't the Bible say that God is always righteous and if you have enough faith then anything is possible? Well, sometimes God does not act in the way we wish. But it is not God's responsibility to act in the way we wish. It is God's world. It is our responsibility to find our place in it. Part of living in God's world is that there will be suffering. The believers will suffer just like the non-believers. But how can a just and righteous God allow there to be suffering in the world? The next chapter addresses this question.

8 SUFFERING

I had many questions about Christianity before becoming a believer, but one of them wasn't about suffering. As someone who didn't grow up going to church, I did not find the idea of suffering to be problematic. It seemed natural to me. The world was inhabited by human beings. These human beings didn't always treat one another kindly. There was suffering because there were human beings. When I heard about the all-loving God, I still didn't question why there was suffering in the world. Some people do struggle with the idea that there is an all-loving God and that there can also be suffering in the world. They feel that somehow an all-loving God would not allow suffering to occur. Their argument does make sense. Would you hurt someone you loved? Perhaps if it was in their best interest you would. I am thinking about someone who is in an abusive relationship, either with another person, drugs, alcohol, or some other abusive substance, when I refer to hurting someone because it would be in their best interest. The emotional, and sometimes physical, pain that comes with the break-up of one of these relationships is sometimes intense. In the end though, the break-up is for the best. So does God allow us to suffer because it is in our best interest? It would be hard to argue that in the case of a child who has cancer. So why does God allow people to suffer if He is always loving?

First, there are two kinds of suffering. One is man-made. This would include crimes such as rape, murder, and blackmail. The second form of suffering will be called natural suffering. This is the type of suffering that comes from nature. Examples include natural disasters and diseases, such as the child who has cancer.

Man-made suffering is simpler to understand. In the beginning, God created Adam and Eve. He created them in His image. He also blessed them with free will. This means that instead of creating automations, which is what He could have done, God decided to give human beings the ability to choose their thoughts and actions. The world is a lot more delightful since it is filled with thinking creatures. If the world were filled with a group of robots then it would be more predictable, but it would also be a lot more boring. Just think of your computer. You like it because it does what you tell it to do. Although there might be some times when you get frustrated because you believe it is not doing what you want, that is mainly due to human error. A computer is predictable. It turns on when you push the power button. It opens a program when you click. It behaves how you want it to. Would you like to have an in-depth conversation with a computer? How about observing a group of computers together? That would be boring. God could have made humans like computers. They could only work when he wanted them to. Instead, he gave us free will to make our own decisions.

He also gave humans a set of opposites. Humans have the capacity to love and hate, laugh and cry. For example, He gave us the desire to eat food. This hunger is contrasted with starvation. It is up to the individual human being to decide if they want to eat or starve. If they choose to starve for too long then they will die. The same is true of the other opposite emotions. A human can choose to love others or hate others. There is a great deal of love capable in the human heart. Jesus is the easiest example of this capacity to love. He loved each and every person he met. He was certainly tested though.

His disciples weren't the most perceptive, especially Peter. Peter was always the first to speak, even when he wasn't asked. He was always impulsive. This impulsiveness would have gotten quite annoying. For instance, on the night of the Last Supper, Jesus got down on his knees and washed the feet of his disciples. Typically this was a job reserved for a servant. It was demeaning. The person had to get down on their knees, in an act of submission. They had to wash another person's feet, which would have been dirty since the people in Israel during the first century only wore sandals. Plus, they were in the desert, so the feet would be covered in sand. Yet, Jesus got down on his knees and washed everybody's feet. His disciples protested. The job was demeaning for their leader, but none of them offered to switch places with Jesus. When Peter asked why Jesus was doing this demeaning task, Jesus replied that it was because he was washing the sin from them. Then Peter said that if Jesus was washing sin from them that he, Peter, wished to be immersed completely in water. Peter always took it to the extreme. The feet washing incident is just one of the examples included in the Gospels. It is comments like this that would make it difficult to be in Peter's presence for three years like Jesus was. Peter's propensity for the extreme had to be annoying. For people like Andrew, his brother, and James and John, who worked with Peter prior to becoming disciples, Peter's impulsivity was normal. They'd been around him since childhood and were used to his ways. The rest of Jesus' disciples were not followers for as long as the four just mentioned. They probably were annoyed with Peter's behavior, but Jesus was the one who had put up with it for the longest. Yet Jesus never showed annoyance because he is love.

Human history is filled with other people who have a great capacity for love. In fact, the majority of humanity displays love on a daily basis. It is unfortunate that the more well-known people of the world happen to be those who choose to hate.

Some do choose to hate, and those who hate can live long lives, see Mao Zedong or Joseph Stalin. They lived long lives in which they were able to persecute people. What was their punishment? Well, their lives could not have been all that great. Since they were dictators who came to power through violence, they would have to constantly look over their shoulder for potential rivals who wanted to kill them and take their place. That could not be good for a night's sleep. But you want them to be punished more, don't you? They killed thousands of their own people simply because they did not share the same beliefs. This is the unfortunate part of human free will. There will be suffering in this world. Perhaps Mao, Stalin, and their ilk did not suffer much more than a bad night's sleep on occasion. But where are they now? You would reply that they are dead. They are dead and buried and can't do any more harm. That is good, but that is not enough. What about all those innocent people? Where is the justice for them? Their justice comes after they die.

One of the first reasons why people decide to believe in God and Christianity is self-preservation. They are not completely sure what happens to them when they die. Do they just sleep for the rest of eternity? Or is there something else? Is there really a heaven and hell.

The world makes a lot more sense if there is a heaven and hell. Heaven and hell are places we go after we die. We spend the rest of eternity in one of those places. All of eternity is a great deal of time. It is a lot more than the small amount of time we spend on Earth. If we only spend a small amount of time on Earth, then it makes sense that God would allow there to be suffering. It might be tough and difficult, but it is only for a short amount of time. The reward for suffering is eternity in heaven. We will not be seeing Mao or Stalin or any of their ilk in heaven. They will be in hell. Justice comes for them after they die.

So God allows us to have free will. We can use our free will to love or we can use our free will to hate. We have the option to do each. If we choose to love, then we are rewarded for eternity by going to heaven. If we choose to hate, then we spend time in hell. The choice is ours. We control what we do in this world, but God will have the final say on where we go for all of eternity. It is a beautiful system when you are able to expand your mind from the here and now of our earthly lives.

So the first form of suffering involves free will. What about the second form – natural suffering? Where is the free will in the child who has cancer or the person who is caught in a mud slide? Doesn't God control these natural events? If He does, then why does He allow human beings to suffer if He is full of love? Let me start with natural disasters.

Natural disasters are caused by the forces of the world around us. Shifts in tectonic plates cause earthquakes. Lightning can spark wildfires that destroy underbrush, forests, and man-made structures. Hurricanes develop in the ocean and destroy anything that stands in the way of the storm's wind and rain. Destruction and death caused by these natural disasters are attributed to nature. These are hazards outside of human control in this world. Living on this Earth exposes you to these hazards. Sometimes these hazards lead to death. In the non-believer way of thinking, nature is the killer and there is no way to avoid it.

For the believer, God is nature. The causes of an earthquake, lighting caused wildfire, or hurricane can be explained in the same way as they are for the non-believer. Science is just a way for humans to explain God's world. The difference between the believer and the non-believer is that the believer cannot just chalk the death and destruction from a natural disaster to chance. God does not work that way. As an all-seeing, all-knowing entity, God does not take chances. God is always in charge. He might work in ways that we do not understand. These ways are typically given names, such as chance, coincidence, or karma. They all go back to God though. So how can it be justified that God allows natural disasters to kill innocent people?

If there is any benefit to a natural disaster, it can be that the event brings everybody in the community together. Disregarding for a moment the deaths, a hurricane or tornado can work to bring people from various walks of lives together. It happens over and over again. You may see a disaster strike one part of the country. You see the devastation. There are homes and businesses destroyed. People are homeless. Children have lost their parents. Volunteers immediately get out to the devastated sites and help out. They provide the basic essentials of life: food, clothing, medicine, shelter, and love. They provide direct help to those in need. Now if you are sitting at home and are unable to help at the scene of the devastation, you can make a donation to those organizations that are directly helping people. By making a donation, you are able to chip-in and help those in need. The great thing about the helping of one another after a natural disaster is that the help transcends all our differences. The old, the poor, minorities, and those of different religions are all pitching in and helping. The old, the poor, minorities, and those of different religions are all being helped. A natural disaster does not discriminate in its destruction. God does not discriminate period. When you help those affected by a natural disaster, you do not discriminate.

At one point in Jesus' ministry, a priest acknowledges that Jesus is a wise man. It is a rarity in the Gospels for a priest to acknowledge Jesus being wise. The priests are typically too preoccupied with themselves and protecting themselves to be anything but jealous and hostel toward Jesus. But this priest acknowledges that Jesus is wise, so he asks Jesus what is the most important rule in the Bible. If you have read the Old Testament then you will know that there are more rules in the book than the Ten Commandments. This priest wanted some guidance as to what God thought life boiled down to. Jesus replied that the purpose of life was to love God and love others. Imagine that; out of all those rules in the Bible it all boils down to those two things.

Love God and love others. It seems easy. Yet do we really follow those two rules? We don't. Not everyone loves God. That is fine. You have free will. If you choose to love God then you will live a better and more rewarding life. It is your choice. Loving others is also a choice. Unfortunately, we do not make the right choice to love others sometimes. We cut people off in traffic. We are afraid of those who look different from us. We ruthlessly compete against co-workers. We exploit those who we feel are weaker. For what gain? The gain is purely material and it is purely in the here and now. We do not take the time to look at the big picture. The big picture only becomes clear during times of great stress. This is the benefit of the natural disaster. When you see people lose everything they have, you get to appreciate what you have. You are able to band together with other people and help those who need help. In short, you are able to love those who experience the natural disaster. For survivors of the natural disaster, the love is direct. Survivors come together to provide food and shelter for one another. There is a great deal of thankfulness from the survivors. They are happy to be alive. They are happy that loved ones are alive. It is too bad that this spirit of community and unity is only temporary. As soon as the story leaves the news cycle, it is back to snipping and cutting people off in traffic for those not in the disaster area. The sense of community is still there in the places effected by the natural disaster, but it soon breaks down as well. There will be yearly remembrances for those who have died, but over time the communal ties loosen.

The only explanation for this breakdown in loving others is that we are human beings. As human beings we are preoccupied with our own little world, goals, and lives. We can only see the short term. When a natural disaster occurs, our short term goal turns to survival. We join together to survive. Once the immediate threat has passed and life returns to some semblance of normalcy, then we disband. We no longer need other people because we live in our own worlds.

The necessity of the natural disaster to bring human beings together is a sad commentary on the state of human free will. We can choose to love others, like we do in the wake of a natural disaster, but we don't. We don't do it every day and because of that we need natural disasters to point out what is important in life.

You might be with me regarding the necessity of natural disasters because of their effects on survivors, but why do so many innocent people have to die? Can't God bring people together without having innocents die? I believe this happens because of the short amount of time we spend on Earth versus spending all eternity in heaven. As humans we consider life to be precious and important. We are small minded. We feel that if we do well at our jobs or make a lot of money then our lives will be meaningful. Perhaps you have different ideas of a meaningful life, which might include raising successful children. Whatever your definition of success in life, it is probably wrong. Jesus said the purpose of life is to love God and love others. If you love God then you are guaranteed a spot in heaven. A spot in heaven lasts for eternity. A life on Earth can be short or last as long as 115 or so years. That is nothing compared to eternity. So if we could love God and love others while on Earth then we will have lived a successful life. For those who are victims of natural disasters, they will be on their way to heaven if they have loved God during their earthly lives. We may mourn those who have died so suddenly, but we shouldn't. Those who die in natural disasters are headed to heaven. That should be celebrated. The suddenness of the death might make us mourn, but after the initial shock, there should be a celebration of the person's earthly life and for their new life in heaven.

Natural disasters are not the only acts of nature that can suddenly take a loved one away from us. Let's look at disease now. Diseases afflict everybody. They do not discriminate against black or white, male or female, young or old, gay or straight, Christian or atheist. If a loved one dies from a disease, the effect on survivors is different depending on the dead person's age.

If an old person is afflicted with a disease and dies it is not treated as a tragedy. There is still pain, but the survivors believe that the person who died lived a long and full life. Eventually an old person will pass away. For instance, in my own family my grandmother was afflicted with lung cancer. Doctors gave her five years to live. She lived for nearly ten years with the disease. Her quality of life got progressively worse, but she still remained cognizant throughout her sickness. So when she died, we did not look at her death as a tragedy. We celebrated the fact that she lived for a long time and was able to accomplish what she wished during her lifetime.

At the same time, her death allowed us to get together as a family. Much like a community that comes together during a natural disaster, families can come together over the sickness of a loved one. This is especially true if the disease is slow acting. The family is able to be at the bedside of the loved one afflicted with the disease. They can spend final moments with the person about to die. But the family can also spend time together. Relatives must be nice to one another when someone is close to death. It wouldn't be socially acceptable to be at the throat of the aunt you hate when your uncle is on his death bed. So once again, God is able to demonstrate the importance of loving others in life. This is one of the benefits to the suffering we feel when someone has a disease. The person who has the disease will eventually die, but they are comforted by the love from those who they have been closest to throughout their life. I remember my grandmother received visits from neighbors and friends she hadn't talked to in a long time. Although she didn't survive the cancer, she was made as comfortable as possible by those she knew best.

What about a child who has leukemia? Does this child deserve to die? The death of a young child due to disease might be the single biggest reason why human beings do not believe in God. There is no community building when a child dies. There is only mourning and questioning about why this horrible event happened.

The standard answer I've heard has been that God has other plans for the child or that the child is now in a better place. I used to think this was a terrible attempt at comfort from ignorant people just trying to push their religion. Now I do agree that the child is going to be in heaven, having never had an opportunity to choose to follow God. What about the parents of the child? There is no benefit to them like there is for survivors of a natural disaster or those who are able to be at the side of a loved one who has lived a long life.

It is difficult to get past the hurt of a dead child. If the parents are able to get past this hurt, they might find a reason for why their child died. It goes back to the idea that the child is in a better place. It also goes back to the idea that there will be suffering on this Earth. The reasons behind this suffering go deeper than this Earth and this human life. The death of a child allows for the parents to think about the big picture. It also allows the others who are affected by the death to look at the big picture. Instead of wallowing in their own pain, which is understandable, the parents can eventually use this tragic event as an opportunity to gain clarity as to the workings of the world and our place in it.

As stated above, God is more concerned with the big picture. He knows that humans will have eternal life. He gave them the free will to choose to believe in Him and go to heaven after they die on Earth. The death of a child can spur parents or other loved ones to reconsider the meaning of their Earthly lives. They can think through why their child died. Their child is in heaven because death came before the child was able to make the decision to choose or not to choose to follow God. The parents still have that choice to make.

Here is how their reasoning can go. The death of a child drives home the idea that life is short. It can also point out that life is precious and that it can end at any time. These ideas all go together. Some will misinterpret this and believe that you have to live so that every moment counts. This is valuable advice if we only have this Earthly life. In other words, if there is no heaven, then it is perfectly reasonable to say that you have to live and appreciate each and every moment because you do not know when you are going to die. But do we really follow this advice of living life to the fullest? Take a look at your daily life. There is a ton of wasted time. You waste time in traffic while you go to work. You waste time in traffic when you leave work. You waste time at work. This time wasting can range from day-dreaming to waiting for the copier to make copies. You waste a lot of time in your daily life. If you are supposed to live each and every moment to the fullest then why are you sitting in traffic each day? But if there is more than this earthly life, if there is a heaven and hell, then you can waste time. Heaven and hell exist because if they didn't then the earthly world would be miserable. It would be full of wasted time and children who die.

Although suffering is a part of life on Earth, it does not have to be a reason for you to doubt the existence of God. God looks at the larger picture. Humans tend to only look at what is immediately in front of them. They see natural disasters and the tragic deaths of children and they ask why an all-loving God would allow these events to take place. If they take a step back from their immediate emotions, they would see that there is some good that comes out of tragic situations. This has a lot to do with the fact that there really is a heaven and hell in which humans will spend eternity after they die on Earth.

9 HEAVEN AND HELL

Heaven and hell give us all sorts of images. Heaven is above us and hell is below. There are angels playing harps on white clouds in heaven. People burn for eternity in hell while the devil delights in their misery. The imagery is distinct, but is it accurate? What about the concepts of heaven and hell? Is there really a heaven? Is there really a hell?

Human beings have probably thought more about what happens to us after we die than any other question. The first humans buried their dead. This proves that early human beings were concerned with what happened after they died. Did they live in some other world? The ancient Egyptians buried their pharaohs with every conceivable need in the afterlife. The same is true of the ancient Chinese and their emperors. As described in Chapter 4, the ancient Jews would bury their dead immediately after death and then wait a year before going to collect the bones for a more permanent resting place. The universality of thinking about what happens after death is one of the reasons why religion must be true.

So, it is no surprise that Christianity would have concepts about what happens after people die. Christians believe that after you die you will either spend eternity in heaven or hell. You want to be in heaven. In fact, there are some people who choose to become Christians solely because you cannot go to heaven unless you are a believer. Once these new converts have their fire insurance, they should be able to completely follow Jesus. Sure there will be the occasional phony Christian, but it is difficult to go to church each and every week of the year and not believe that Jesus of Nazareth was the Son of God or that the world is run by God. It is those who attend at Christmas and Easter, and believe that because they attend that they have fire insurance, who are the phonies and might find themselves locked out of heaven.

If you have made it this far though, there is a good chance that you are more than a Christmas and Easter Christian. You might have gotten interested in Christianity because of the concepts of heaven and hell, but now you realize that there is more to it and that the other benefits of Christianity are better than the fire insurance you originally wanted. That is why this chapter on heaven and hell is near the back of the book. There is a great deal more to God then just what happens after we die.

The case for eternal life was briefly outlined in the previous chapter. We all know that we are going to die one day. Some of us die a few minutes after we've been born, others 115 years after we are born. The majority of us will die somewhere between those two extremes. Now if you are an atheist you believe that your life ends when you die. The lights are turned off and your flesh will rot until you are bones and then the bones turn to dust. It is no wonder that atheists are so angry. They have nothing to look forward to once they die and their lives are filled with the suffering and angst that comes with living on this Earth. I know that I would be mad if my ancestors rose out of the slime of some exceptionally hot pool only to evolve into human beings so obsessed with paper currency and plastic cards.

A lot that we take for granted in a twenty-first century capitalistic society would not exist if there was only this life on Earth. For one, there is the concept of money. What is money? Originally human beings had the barter system. If you had something I wanted and I had something you wanted then we could trade those two items. The barter system was necessary because no individual could produce everything he might need in life. As the system became more complex, meaning the trades became more than one item for one item, there needed to be a value system. Not only was a value system important for the exchange of goods, but it also helped centralize power in a society. A government could create a system of money, coins for example, and anyone in their realm of power would have to use this system in order to trade. The money system was developed because only a strong central power could create coins and enforce their value. As human society developed, a simple coin system evolved into a more complex monetary system. Paper bills were introduced. In the twentieth century, countries started to leave the gold standard. This basically meant that instead of having the paper stand in for a valuable metal, the paper was given an arbitrary value based on the number printed on the bank note. Today, it seems as if money is only a series of numbers on a computer screen. Workers receive direct deposits in their bank accounts. We use debit and credit cards that are tied to the digits in our bank account. When we buy something the digits go down. When we make money the digits go up. What is their value now?

So how does this relate to eternal life? Well, the monetary system is basically pointless if all we have is this life on Earth. If there is no eternity then there shouldn't be a monetary system. As stated above, the barter system originally had a purpose when it was a one-for-one trade. As soon as central governments developed the coin system to enhance their power, we lost the most important part of the barter system. The barter system was designed to help each and every person get what they wanted. The money system that exists in the twenty-first century only encourages people to acquire more numbers on their computer bank accounts. But this is alright because this earthly life isn't all there is. The inefficiency of the monetary system, where a few have all the money and the majority have little money is just one example of why there is more than just our earthly life.

If we just had our earthly life then I can guarantee you that I would not have written this book. There are more interesting ways I could spend my limited time on Earth. I would love to see the world. Seeing the natural wonders of the world and the man-made wonders of the world are at the top of my bucket list. I would love to see the animals that inhabit the Earth with us. Seeing a lion in the wild or a herd of buffalo would be amazing. Now these are just some of the sights I would like to see if I knew that my life was limited to the short amount of time I spent on Earth. You may have some other goals. Unfortunately, we are all forced to work for money in order to pay for items. Many of these items are unnecessary. Insurance for instance. You basically pay money for more money when you purchase insurance. It should be unnecessary for the survival of a human being. However, it is an absolute necessity for someone living in a modern society.

I am not trying to bad-mouth capitalism or advocate for an overthrow of the system. I don't particularly care because there is more to life on Earth and eternity than money. I just wish to point out the inefficiency of the system. The cavemen didn't use a monetary system and they lasted for thousands of years. If you think the cavemen are an inadequate example since we are so far advanced technologically, then think of your ideal society. Think about all the pictures of utopia that you've seen. Do any of those involve money? Is a utopian society one in which everybody is a millionaire? I have never heard of one described in such a way. Most utopian societies involve everybody pitching in to help one another. There is no war. There is no exploitation. Everyone treats their neighbor as they wish to be treated. It is a lofty picture and one that we will never be able to reach on this Earth. But we will be able to reach it in eternity. A great deal of the pictures of a utopian society are similar to the images conjured when someone describes heaven.

Let us start with what heaven is not. The popular image of heaven involves people dressed in white, floating on clouds and playing the harp. Cartoons we see as children do a good job of implementing this image in our heads. There is a great deal of violence in cartoons. When a cartoon character dies, they can't just be dropped in the ground and have a sad funeral. Instead, they are shown ascending to heaven where they float on a cloud and play the harp. This is the first images of heaven we gain and then we don't get much for the rest of our lives. Oddly enough, the Bible is relatively silent regarding the specifics of heaven.

Some who have been declared legally dead but come back to us will report that they have seen a brilliant white light. This white light is most likely purgatory, the place where you go prior to entering heaven or hell. Still, heaven is associated with white. White is the color of purity and we associate white with that which is good. Jesus is typically pictured as wearing a white robe. So heaven is associated with white. Heaven is also associated with being above us.

Jesus is said to have ascended to heaven. In the Old Testament, the prophet Isaiah also ascended to heaven. Even the ancient Romans believed that their emperors ascended to heaven after they died. Nobody ever descended to heaven. Heaven has always been looked at as being above us. Part of this can be explained by the fact that human beings have remained firmly on the ground for the majority of their history. It wasn't until the twentieth century that air and space flight were developed. So it was natural that people would think heaven was above them. The image of people floating on clouds fits with this idea. Of course with the technological innovations of the twentieth century, the popular image of heaven as being in the clouds has dissipated.

Jesus mentions the coming of the Kingdom of Heaven quite frequently. There are other mentions of heaven throughout the Bible, but nothing that gives us a concrete idea of what heaven is like. All that is clear is you want to be in heaven. Part of the reason is because Jesus says you want to be in heaven. As a wise teacher, not to mention being the Son of God, you would listen to Jesus and when he says that you want to be in heaven then you want to be in heaven. Heaven is where God resides. Heaven is full of glory and peace and happiness and any other positive adjective that you can think of. But what does heaven physically look like? What will you look like? You've just died. Will you retain your human image? Will it be the image of you when you died or will it be the image of you when you were twenty-three? Or will you get a new body? The possible answers to these questions are the stuff of science fiction writers. As human beings, we will not know for sure what heaven looks like until we arrive, but I will tell you how I see it.

To me, heaven will be something like the Garden of Eden. The Garden of Eden seemed to be heaven on Earth. Anything Adam and Eve could have wanted was available to them. There was just one rule and when they broke that rule they got kicked out of Eden. Now, heaven probably exists in a separate plane that we can only enter once we die. This plane will look a great deal like Earth. This makes sense as it will be familiar to humans who have lived on Earth. There will be no war, no pestilence, no petty fighting, no exploitation. It will be the utopian society humans have thought and dreamed of for a long time. More importantly, heaven will be populated with others. It will not be sparsely populated like the Garden of Eden. Every human being who has believed in God from the beginning of time will be there. That means that you will be there will all the great figures of the past. From the first disciples of Jesus, to Bach, on through the Founding Fathers of the United States, to Florence Nightingale, Martin Luther King Jr., Johnny Cash, and Desmond Tutu. There will be your relatives who went to church each and every Sunday. Of course there will also be God.

Although there are a ton of benefits to being a Christian, having the opportunity to meet God might be the best reason to believe in Christianity. Certainly treating others the way you wish to be treated is worthwhile. Of course there is also eternal life in heaven once you die. But really, being able to meet God is perhaps the greatest reward to being a Christian. Just think of it. You will be able to meet the one who created you. He created the Earth you've walked on for many years. He created the people you interacted with on a daily basis. He created those who you loved and those who annoyed you. He created the sun that provided light to you each day. He created the stars that you looked at each night. He's the one who gave humans the ability to reason and think scientifically. He is the one who gave us the free will to act how we wish. He is the one who gave us the ability to love. Once you get to heaven you get to meet this creator face-to-face. The thought of being able to have a face-to-face conversation with someone that powerful and great is just overwhelming. What will you say to God when you meet face-to-face? Personally, I plan on not speaking until being spoken to. I'm naturally a quiet person. For me it isn't so much conversations that are important, but rather the presence of another human being. I will just be happy to stand in the presence of God's glory when I reach heaven.

Not everyone is going to be able to experience the emotions of standing in God's glory though. We each have a choice to make. We can choose to believe in God, or we can dismiss it all as just a cult or some superstition that was created thousands of years ago before humans developed modern reasoning skills. If you choose to believe in God though, you will be rewarded by getting to meet God in heaven. Choosing to follow God so that you can meet Him face-to-face later on should be one of the biggest accomplishments of your life. Jesus and the other prophets found in the Bible understood this. That is part of the reason why they encourage people to follow God, the other being the short-term benefits that belief can have on your Earthly life. This is also one of the reasons why there is not a great deal of description of heaven in the Bible. What heaven looks like physically doesn't matter because you are going to get to meet the creator of everything. If God wants heaven to have a brown sky one day and a green sky the next, or no sky at all, then He is able to do so. Therefore, why waste words on heavenly descriptions when the most important part of getting to heaven is that you are going to meet God.

The powerful appeal of heaven is sometimes overshadowed by a greater aversion to hell. Some people choose to believe in Christianity, not because of God and a love for God, but because they do not wish to burn in hell for eternity. But is hell all fire and suffering?

If there is little physical description of heaven in the Bible, then there is even less of hell. The popular image of people suffering in fire for all of eternity comes to us courtesy of the Middle Ages in Europe. This was considered a dark period in human civilization, although civilization was thriving at this time in the Middle East and Asia. The fall of the Roman Empire brought a long period of instability to Europe. There was internal conflict among a large number of feudal lords on the European continent. Externally, the Muslims were threatening to conquer all of Europe and replace Christianity with a new religion. Out of this fear came pictures of hell that emphasized suffering. Eternal burning in flames would greet those in Europe who did not believe in God. In this battle for good and evil during Medieval Europe, it was clear that the bad forces of Islam and internal war were winning. It would take divine intervention from God to save the Europeans from a hell on Earth. This hell on Earth never transpired and after rebuffing Muslim advances in Europe, and the feudal kingdoms evolving into nations, Europe entered the Renaissance. Still, the image of hell as being full of horrendous suffering persisted. It is even used today in churches.

Another reason why hell is popularly pictured as being full of fire is because it is supposed to be below us. Since we know that the Earth is full of molten rock, it makes sense that hell is filled with fire. But this idea that hell is below us in the Earth is false. We would have found hell with our scientific equipment if it existed anywhere between the surface of the Earth. We have found no evidence of there being a hell anywhere inside the Earth. Now that doesn't mean that hell isn't going to have fire, it just means hell isn't located within the Earth. Of course you should have known that after our discussion of heaven. Heaven is not visible to us above the Earth, so why should hell be visible to us below?

Instead, hell is probably in some alternate plane like heaven. Our knowledge of what God has created is extremely limited. It is mostly confined to knowledge of our own planet. Just because we haven't found a heaven or hell doesn't mean that it doesn't exist. Still, if you listen to the speeches of some pastors on Sundays, it sounds like hell will soon engulf the Earth no matter where it is located.

The fire and brimstone speeches are used to whip Christians back on the road to Christ and good living. This can be an effective tool, but it is not an accurate depiction of hell. Although I have never been to hell, nor do I know anyone who has, it does not make reasonable sense that hell would be full of eternal suffering. Remember that God is love. God loves each and every one of us. He bestowed us with free will so that we can pick and choose our thoughts. We can choose to love others, including God. If we choose not to love or believe in God then we will spend eternity in hell. But God isn't vengeful enough to carry on a grudge for all of eternity. He is a just and righteous God full of love. As such, he would never allow one of His free-willed creations to burn in hell for eternity. Now, God can also get angry and I am sure He is angry and disappointed when one of His creations ignores Him. So it would not be a surprise that in God's anger, there will be some suffering in hell for those who do not believe. A thousand years of burning in hell is a great deal of time to us as humans. To God, a thousand years is not a great deal of time. Compared to eternity, a thousand years is not a long time. So you could burn in hell for a thousand years for rejecting God, but you will not spend eternity burning in hell because God is love and just. That might seem contradictory to you right now, but by taking a step back and considering just how long eternity is, you will understand how a God full of love could allow one of His creations to suffer for a thousand years and still be called just.

So if hell isn't below us and we do not suffer for all of eternity in flames, then how will those who choose to reject God live in hell? There are almost as many different depictions of hell as there is of heaven – perhaps even more. Thinking about the evils of hell can be much more interesting than dreaming about the ideal society found in heaven. C.S. Lewis depicted hell as a place of extreme isolation. Now if you are an introvert like me then you might not mind being isolated from other people. It could actually be considered a sort of heaven. But in Lewis' hell, there is no real chance for human interaction. Each person lives alone in their own mansion. Their closest neighbor is miles away. Their only real chance of human interaction is talking to themselves or watching their neighbors with a telescope. Of course a long walk would lead one to the doorstep of their neighbor. But there is not a lot of this in Lewis' hell. Everyone is too self-absorbed to want to deal with their neighbors. So Lewis' hell features people living in mansions, widely dispersed from each other, and completely self-absorbed. Some might say that is already how certain societies on Earth act.

The ideas of self-absorption and fake luxury tend to run through many depictions of hell from the twentieth century. In a *Twilight Zone* episode, creator Rod Serling postulated that hell is a place where all your dreams come true. "A Nice Place to Visit" revolves around a petty thief who ends up being shot by the police when a robbery goes wrong. He wakes up in what he believes to be heaven. It is heaven for him. As a petty thief he is given all his wants: money, women, and drinks. He wants to go gambling. It turns out the games are rigged so that he will always win. He is able to rob banks and not get caught. This goes well for about a week. Then it becomes boring. Our hero complains to the man who brought him there that he wishes he were in hell instead of heaven. The thief is informed that he is in hell. Hell for Serling is a place where all your dreams do come true, but they might not always turn out to be what you really wanted.

It is an interesting theme for Serling to pursue. Interesting because we typically will believe in God if God were to give us everything we wanted. God is not Santa Claus. He is not a slot machine. You cannot ask Him for anything you want and then say that you will believe in Him once He does something to help you. God does not work that way. Serling might be saying that the devil works this way instead.

Now the above portrayals of hell could be as far off as the Middle Age pictures of eternal burning. For someone raised at the end of the twentieth century though, I tend to find the pictures Lewis and Serling created to be more accurate. However, none of us will ever know for sure what heaven or hell is like until we die. One of the topics not discussed in this chapter regarding heaven and hell are the inhabitants of those regions. Sure there is God in heaven and Satan in hell, but what about angels and demons? Do they really exist?

10 ANGELS AND DEMONS

I will tell you straight out that I have some serious doubts as to the existence of angels and demons and there being an eternal struggle between the two. It seems a little much to me to have to believe in some unseen war between angels and demons. It is like something out of science fiction. At least, that is what I imagine it to be.

I do want to make it clear that despite my doubts on this subject, I have no doubts about God or Christianity being true. It is healthy to have doubts. You may not have doubts on this subject, but on some other subject contained in this book. I have included this subject because you need to know that it's alright to have doubts. You also don't have to throw away all that you believe in just because you have doubts about a minor portion of Christianity. So this chapter will include my doubts while examining angels, demons, and the most difficult book in the Bible – Revelations.

An angel is supposed to be someone dressed in white with wings. I tend to think of an angel as someone who is larger than a normal human being, perhaps as much as seven feet tall. Why I have this idea I'm not sure. Maybe it has to do with the authority angels are supposed to have. I associate height with authority. To me, a demon is a small creature, but one that is full of viciousness. He typically runs around with horns and a pitch fork with smaller wings on his back.

Now regarding this struggle between angels and demons, I think of a group of demons swarming around one angel or an army of angels attempting to eradicate thousands of demons. There is a lot of gore in this struggle. Angels die. Demons die. It isn't pretty, just like any other war. Yet somehow human beings are unable to see this struggle. This is too much for me to believe. I cannot understand how a gory war can be going on around us and we cannot see it.

Now I have also heard that this war is more of a psychological battle between good and evil. The battlefield is actually the mind of human beings and the victors get the human's soul for eternity. You have seen portrayals of this struggle via the angel on one shoulder and the demon appearing on the other shoulder. It is supposed to be a visual example of the debate raging in our conscience, but it might actually be what is really happening inside us. In the portrayals, the angel makes the case for being good and staying the course. The demon entices us with material dreams and riches. In the end the person in the movie, cartoon, or television show will typically choose to follow what the demon says. The idea behind this being that the larger picture of the story will include a moral that shows the person who chose the demon that he was wrong. As nice as this is as an example, it isn't always that simple in real life. There is no angel or demon that appears on our shoulders each time there is a tough decision to be made. There really isn't even a clear-cut good or bad option in most decisions. The decisions we make are filled with gray areas. That is one of the reasons why it is so difficult to believe in angels and demons. If everything was clear cut then it would be easy to point toward the good as being the decision the angel wants you to take and the bad being the one the demon wants you to take.

The Bible unequivocally states that angels exist. Angels appear several times in the Old Testament and the New Testament. The angel Gabriel appears to Mary to tell her that she is carrying God's child. He also foretells the birth of John the Baptist. In the Old Testament he appears to King David. So what does this all mean? Well, it means that angels appear to human beings. Angels also seem to have some individuality if they are given names. Gabriel also appears to be the leader of the angels or he is the greatest angel since he is the one who is constantly named in the Bible. Finally, angels are messengers of God. They appear to humans in order to give them a message from God. Why God chose angels to deliver messages instead of resorting to the burning bush like He did with Moses is unknown.

What form angels take is also unknown. It does not appear that they are harp players dressed in white and have large wings. Instead, they appear to be quite frightening. The first phrase out of any angel's mouth is some variation of "Do not be afraid." This could be because the angel is physically intimidating. Like I mentioned above, my view of an angel is something that is quite taller than a typical human being. Or this introduction might be made because the angel suddenly appears out of thin air. There is no warning before an angel appears. Certainly finding an angel next to you when you thought you were alone would be frightening. Although the angel who appeared before Jesus' disciples after his ascension to heaven did not tell the disciples to be unafraid. They could have been so much in awe already at the tomb being empty that the typical angel greeting would be redundant. Whatever the case, angels appear out of thin air and give instructions from God to human beings.

Luckily for you and me, angels do not appear to everybody. I know I would be terrified if an angel appeared before me. It wouldn't so much be because of the angel's presence, but because of the angel's message. An angel only appears when God wants someone to do something. The angel told the disciples to spread the gospel. Gabriel informed Mary that she was not to worry about being pregnant despite being a virgin because she was having the Lord's child. So with this in mind, my natural reaction to seeing an angel would be fear. Out of the billion Christians on this planet, God chose me to do something for Him. I would rebel and try to talk the angel out of delivering the message because I would be scared out of my mind. As a human, I do not feel that I can do more than God, so it is difficult for me to fathom how I could help God out. But in the end, I would certainly accept the angel's message and do God's will. It isn't so much that I would be afraid of punishment for not listening to the angel, see the story of Jonah for an example of what happens when you rebel against God's requests, but I would accept because I would have the power of God behind me. If God asks me directly to do something, then I know that I will have His backing. He will be there for me every step of my mission. God's a pretty powerful ally to have. So after initially whining to the angel about my situation, I would be ecstatic about having the full support of God behind me.

Oddly enough, I do not feel that I would have the same fear I have for angels if I were visited by a demon. This is because I would also know that I had the full support of God behind me. God will not let me fall to a demon, so I would not be terrified if visited by a demon or even Satan himself.

Now Satan's an interesting figure. In the popular imagination, Satan is the caretaker of hell. He is a muscular red man with horns and a pitchfork. He is pure evil and takes great delight in suffering. This image is hard to believe. A blood red man walking around with pitchfork, horns, and cape is more likely to be found at a Halloween party than walking down the street in twenty-first century America. Fortunately, the Bible clarifies Satan's image.

Satan makes a few memorable appearances in the Bible. His longest appearance comes in Revelations, which I will address below. Perhaps his best known appearance is in Genesis with Adam and Eve. He appears to Eve in serpent form and convinces her to eat from the Tree of Knowledge. Now the story goes that Satan was originally an angel, but he rebelled against God. He wanted to be God and when it became clear that he could never be God, Satan rebelled and took delight in all things evil. If Satan really were an angel, then that means angels can shape shift. The angel became a serpent. This also might be a reason why angels give the warning to not be afraid when they first appear. They might not appear in human form.

The oddest appearance of Satan comes from the Book of Job. In the opening chapters, Satan and God have a conversation like they are old friends. God asks Satan what he has been up to and Satan replies that he has been traveling the Earth making life miserable for humans. God takes this in stride and asks Satan if he has heard about how Job has such great faith. Then Satan challenges God by saying that Job would renounce God if Job were given hardships. God accepts Satan's challenge. This is quite the exchange and something that we would not expect from God. If God were really in an eternal battle with Satan, then why is He having such a pleasant conversation with the enemy? Shouldn't God smite Satan like He does His enemies in the Old Testament? Instead, Satan and God converse like they are two golf pros who are arguing about who can hit the ball farther. But God is God. God knows that even if Satan tempts Job or Adam and Eve and even if it appears like Satan wins when Jesus is killed, it is only a false victory. God knows that good will always triumph over evil. He knows that love will conquer hate. He knows and so it doesn't matter what Satan does – Satan will never win. God doesn't need to fight Satan. He just needs to step aside and let Satan defeat himself or get so frustrated that he quits. This is what happens in the Book of Job. Job is able to weather all the evil deeds Satan does to him and still keep faith in God.

Another example occurs when Satan tempts Jesus in the wilderness after Jesus has been baptized. For forty days Satan attempts to get Jesus to renounce God. Jesus doesn't directly fight Satan. Jesus quotes scripture. For each time Satan tempts Jesus, Jesus is there with a Biblical verse to affirm his faith. Jesus is the Son of God. He knows all about Satan. He met him before. Jesus knows that all he has to do is ride out Satan's storm. Satan will eventually get so frustrated that he will leave Jesus alone so that Jesus can complete his mission on Earth. During the Sermon on the Mount, Jesus advises us to turn the other cheek. He acts on his words when he gets tempted by Satan in the wilderness. He turns the other cheek each time Satan attacks. Eventually he outlasts Satan. Just like God in the larger battle, Jesus is able to defeat Satan's temptations. There is no big battle between God and Satan with lots of gore. If anything, it's a psychological war with God frustrating Satan so much that Satan gives up. So when it is said that we are in the midst of an eternal battle between angels and demons that we cannot see, then it must be a psychological war. The Bible points toward this, but as humans our minds think of war in physical terms.

Now it is said that Satan is a selfish angel who rebelled against God. He chose, out of his own free will, to embrace all that is evil. This makes sense and is consistent with the idea of free will as applied to human beings. If human beings are endowed with free will then angels should be as well. There is a problem here though. Satan chose to become evil, but as an all-seeing, all-knowing being, God would know beforehand that Satan would choose evil. God had prior knowledge that Satan would turn on Him, yet He went ahead and created Satan. Doesn't this mean there is a contradiction between free will and prior knowledge?

The typical argument made to consolidate this apparent contradiction between prior knowledge and free will is that those humans who choose not to follow God during their earthly life will not be invited to spend eternity in heaven. This makes sense and is effective and explains why there is suffering in the world. But the issue of Satan is different. Since Satan is an angel, he already possesses eternal life. Therefore, the punishment for choosing not to follow God does not apply to Satan. Instead, Satan is allowed to commit evil acts throughout all of eternity. If the Book of Job is to be believed, then Satan's reign of terror is not limited to the Earth. God resides in heaven and Satan arrives to discuss Job with God. So does this mean their conversation is going on in heaven? If so, why is Satan allowed in heaven? This is where I have my doubts about angels and demons.

Perhaps the biggest problem I have with Christian doctrine is found in the Book of Revelations. It reads like a fictional work. If I had started reading the Bible with the Book of Revelations, I am sure that I would not be a follower of Christ. Revelations is just too far out there for me to believe. It is what critics want to believe about religions. There is so much fantasy that it is tough to describe. Luckily, it is unlike the rest of the Bible. The rest of the Bible is grounded in historical acts that can be verified. Revelations is the story of the apocalypse. Therefore, it cannot be compared with history to verify its accuracy.

It is said that Revelations was written by Jesus' disciple John when he resided on the island of Patmos. Unlike the other books of the New Testament, John states that he is the author and gives his location. This should automatically raise a red flag. As we saw in Chapter 5, many ancient books, especially those claiming to be eyewitness histories, did not include the first person or mention the author except on the tag of the scroll. So for John to mention himself as author is odd. For an author of a previous Gospel to do so is even odder. Why does he refer to himself as the "disciple Jesus loved" in his Gospel, but chooses to use his name at the beginning of Revelations?

After introducing himself, John goes on to write that what follows are a sequence of visions he saw. These visions depict the end of the world with those who believe in Jesus rising up to heaven (the rapture), while those who do not believe are left on the earth to see the final battle between God and Satan. Jesus makes an appearance. Other famous images, such as the Whore of Babylon, the Four Horsemen of the Apocalypse, and the mark of the beast (666) come from Revelations. I would like to go into more detail about the visions in revelations, but I can't make heads or tails out of them. It makes no sense to me. It is like a work of science fiction. Although the images are not necessarily those we associate with science fiction.

This is interesting because we typically associate science fiction with the future. Revelations is supposed to be a picture of the future apocalypse. Now there are books and theories and Internet articles about the predictions in Revelations that have come true or have not come true since it was written. That's fine, but when we read a work of science fiction we expect to read about advanced technology human beings should develop in the future. Where is this advanced technology in the Book of Revelations? Now, apologists will state that John did not understand everything that he saw since he was unfamiliar with the technologies that humans would later develop. This might be true, but what about the Four Horsemen of the Apocalypse? John clearly states that four horsemen appear riding different colored horses. Travel via horse would be the most advanced form of transportation in the first century. Not many people use horses to travel in the twenty-first century. So either all of human technology is eliminated with the rapture, John can't tell the difference between an advanced form of technology and a horse, or John is wrong. I tend to believe that John was wrong. Horses would be looked at as sources of power in the first century. A great deal of those living in the Jewish home land would not have experience with horses. Peasants couldn't afford a horse. The wealthy or Roman cavalry would be the only ones capable of owing a horse. Therefore, the imagery of a horse would be meaningful for those who lived in the first century. The imagery would keep its power until the 1800s when the industrial revolution soon made transportation via horse outdated.

So if John is wrong in Revelations, does that mean the Gospel of John is also wrong? No. As discussed in Chapter 5, the Gospel of John has all the hallmarks we expect to see in an eyewitness account. Besides, the stories of the two books are different. The Gospel of John is intended to portray the life and teachings of Jesus. The Book of Revelations is an attempt at prophecy.

Prophecy is not complex. Just about everyone attempts to predict the future. When you are in school you study diligently for an upcoming test. If you've studied well and feel confident that you know most of the answers to the questions, then you can predict that your future grade is going to be high. This might be too simplistic an example for you. You have a great deal of control of the future in the test example. What about something where you don't have control of events? Well, that's a lot more difficult. When you start to relinquish control of future events then the likelihood of your prophecy coming true goes down. You also run the risk of looking like a crazy person. Take for instance those people who constantly predict the world is going to end. A lot of them get their ideas from the Book of Revelations. They try to fit the apocalyptic prophesy of John into their own worldview. These apocalyptic believers are always wrong, but they do end up getting some media attention. Perhaps that's all they're interested in.

So for me, the Book of Revelations is just another one of the predictions of the world ending. Personally, I don't see the world ending and Jesus coming back in my lifetime. In order for God's plan to take full effect, everybody in the world has to be exposed to Christianity. There are still portions of the world where Christianity has yet to penetrate. Christianity started in the Middle East, spread through Europe, was brought to the Americas in the sixteenth and seventeenth centuries, then made inroads into Africa in the twentieth century. The islands around Southeast Asia have become receptive to Christianity in recent years. It appears that Asia will be the next region of the world in which Christianity will spread. Once this happens then we can discuss the impending apocalypse, but I don't expect that to happen while I'm alive.

Of course I could be wrong about the Book of Revelations. What then? Am I no longer a Christian? Fortunately, Christianity isn't based around belief in Revelations but belief in Jesus. I have my doubts about angels, demons, and the Book of Revelations, but none of these doubts are big enough to overshadow my belief in the historicity of Jesus and that Jesus really was the Son of God.

11 ATHEISM

This whole book has given you reasons for why there is a God. Ultimately though, you have the freedom to choose to believe in God or the freedom not to believe in God. Atheism does not give you this choice. Atheism is a religion that believes that there is only human reason and human science to explain the world around us. Fortunately, reason and science fit in perfectly with Christianity.

My sole attempt in writing this book has been to present some Christian issues in a reasonable and logical fashion. Chapter 4 on the historicity of Jesus and Chapter 5 about the Gospels as eyewitness testimony especially use reason to make their cases. Quite frankly, if Christianity did not stand the test of reason, then I would not be a believer. Where Christianity runs into problems is when the unnatural enters into the land of reason. In the case of the historical Jesus, this is the claim that Jesus is God. Based on the evidence, it is reasonable to believe that Jesus of Nazareth existed. It is also reasonable to state that Jesus of Nazareth was a great spiritual teacher. But to not include God when mentioning his teachings is unfair. It is the Jefferson Bible. Thomas Jefferson thought the Bible was much better if all the miracles were cut out of it, but that isn't fair to the book. You cannot have the great moral teachings without God. To believe otherwise is untruthful.

But what you really want in order to believe is a direct statement from Jesus claiming divinity. Some atheists will point out that Jesus never directly claimed divinity. He never said that he is God. Therefore, if he didn't admit to divinity, he really wasn't God. Christians like Paul who came after Jesus just projected divinity onto Jesus.

It is true that Jesus never flatly stated he was God. However, it can be reasonably deduced based on the evidence that Jesus made claims to divinity. His claims to divinity are most often seen in the Gospel of John.

His biggest claim comes when he debates with the Pharisees. The priests of the day believed that Jesus was demon possessed or even sent from Satan. In response, Jesus claims that it is the Pharisees who were the ones sent from Satan. In contrast, Jesus was sent from God. The Pharisees directly confronted him with questions about how he could possibly remove demons from people if he wasn't from Satan. Jesus responded with the famous "house divided" reason. He could not be Satan because he cast out demons. Instead, he had to be from God because there is no good reason why Satan would want one of his workers to cast out demons that have already been installed in people. A house divided cannot stand, therefore Jesus had to be from something more powerful than Satan. He was from God.

There is also Jesus' great transfiguration. Now the validity of this story can certainly be questioned, but what Jesus asks Peter at the end is completely valid and probably was asked at some point. During a trip to the Mount of Olives, the inner group of Jesus' disciples (Peter, Andrew, James, and John) are present to witness the arrival of Moses and the prophet Elijah. The two great prophets join Jesus in transfiguration. Essentially the transfiguration involved all three men becoming radiant. This story is meant to equate Jesus with the two other prophets in that he is equal to the only man to ascend to heaven without dying (Elijah) and the most important man in Jewish history (Moses). When Jesus' disciples are thoroughly impressed, and the two other prophets have left, Jesus turns to Peter and asks him who people think Jesus is. Peter replies that people believe Jesus is a great prophet. Jesus then asks Peter who Peter thinks Jesus is. Peter replies that he believes Jesus is the Messiah.

Now in modern parlance the terms Messiah, Chosen One, and Son of God are used interchangeably. In ancient times, the Messiah was believed to be someone like King David. King David was a mortal chosen by God to lead God's people into an era of prosperity. The Messiah that the prophets in the Old Testament were describing was going to be another King David. This is one of the reasons why Jews do not believe in Jesus' divinity. Jesus of Nazareth was just another prophet, but he was not the Messiah. Jews are still awaiting their Messiah from God who will lead them to prosperity like King David.

So if Jesus was considered the Messiah (a mortal chosen by God to lead God's people) by his disciples, how did he become divine? Christians believe that Jesus was not just a man, but the Son of God. The reason is because Jesus actively proclaimed to be the Son of God. He used his words and actions to proclaim his divinity. Jesus actually claimed to have the power to forgive sins. In the Jewish belief system, only God can forgive sins. Jesus forgave sins multiple times, but most noticeably when healing a lame man who was dropped down through the roof of a home where Jesus preached. The crowd was amazed that this man, who was unable to walk, was suddenly able to get up and walk after Jesus put his hands on him. What might have been missed by those attending, or those who read the story for the first time, is that Jesus told the man that his sins were forgiven. Jesus also forgave a woman of her sins of prostitution when her village wished to stone her to death. When Jesus forgave sins, he was actively proclaiming the authority of God. This eventually led to his being brought before Pontius Pilate. Only the Roman Emperor could claim divinity. By Jesus claiming to be divine, he was putting himself on the same level as the Roman Emperor. Since there could only be one emperor, the blasphemer (Jesus) had to be crucified.

Besides Jesus' acts, Jesus referred to himself as being divine. He did not use the term Messiah because he was not a normal man chosen by God to lead God's people. Instead, Jesus referred to himself as the Son of Man. Now this term is used in the Old Testament, but there is not a clear picture of what the Son of Man will look like, unlike the Messiah. The Son of Man is similar to the Messiah. He is a chosen one from God who will lead God's people. But Jesus preferred to use the term Son of Man instead of Messiah. Why?

As Christians, we refer to Jesus as the Son of God. Jesus referred to himself as the Son of Man. The two terms are similar, but just a little different. The first words have the same meaning. The word Son in each phrase means that Jesus is subordinate to God the Father while on Earth. As the Son, Jesus and Christians are acknowledging that Jesus was conceived in Mary like any other human being. His mother is Mary. His father is God. He even refers to God as the Father in his teaching. However, he also refers to God being the Father of all humanity. Remember the beginning of the Lord's Prayer? "*Our* Father, who art in heaven." So even though Jesus refers to himself as the Son, we are all offspring of God the Father. This is where the last word in Son of Man comes into play.

Jesus isn't just some half-man, half-God like Heracles from Greek mythology. Jesus is fully divine. However, Jesus was sent by God to atone for humanity's sins. In order to do this, Jesus had to take a human form so that he could die. In order to serve humanity and atone for humanity's sins, Jesus had to become the Son of Man. Man being humanity. The term Son of Man means that the son of God the Father is subordinating himself for humanity's sins so that humans can have eternal life.

The point of the above example is to not only provide additional evidence for Jesus being God, but to demonstrate that a rational argument can be made in favor of Christianity. The only difference in a rational Christian argument and that of an atheist is the Christian is capable of taking the small leap of faith to acknowledge the possibility of there being more than just human beings involved in life on Earth. Although it should be mentioned that to be an atheist you also need to possess faith. You need to have faith in there only being a natural world that we can see and observe and not a spiritual side to the world where a grand creator exists. So either way, a well reasoned argument also needs an element of faith for it to ring true to human beings.

What makes atheists believe that their leap of faith is marginal is the fact that they have science on their side and Christianity does not. Unfortunately, this is not the case. It is popularly portrayed that science and Christianity are on opposite sides. This can be true when it comes to the evolution vs. creationism argument. Another reason for why some believe science and Christianity cannot be compatible is because of the length of time each has been around.

Humans have been religious creatures ever since they existed. Science, on the other hand, is relatively new on the scene. It is an unfortunate assumption that whatever is new is more advanced and since it is more advanced it is superior to what occurred in the past. Religion was great for our ancestors who were unenlightened and needed some explanation for how the natural world worked. Today, we have science to explain everything. Now, science is not always correct. At one time there was a belief that the temperature of the body was controlled by a substance termed caloric. But this is an example from the Middle Ages. We now have modern science. Modern science is based on experiments, observations, and conclusions about the natural world. The scientific method is what defines modern science. Experiments lead to truth. Truth can sometimes lead to disagreements with the authorities. For a great deal of time, in Europe the authorities were Christians. Therefore, in the case of someone like Galileo, pointing out the truth that the planets orbit the sun and not the Earth led to his excommunication from the church. A famous case like this is used by atheists to justify the incompatibility of science and religion.

However, the biggest proponents of the incompatibility of science and religion are Christians not atheists. For some reason Christians are fearful of science. They adhere literally to the Bible and if it is not in the Bible then it does not exist. This is a frustrating and debilitating position to take. Instead of fighting against science, Christians should embrace science. Science is a way that we as human beings can better understand the world God created. The more we learn about the world God created, the more we can appreciate the gift of life. We can also gain a better appreciation of just how precise God really is. There is not a great deal of randomness in the world. The human body is not thrown together in some haphazard way. The same is true of the trees, grass, animals, oceans, and weather of this Earth. When you look at the world as described through science, it becomes clear that the odds of everything turning out just the way they did through some random process is very low. Lower than the probability that God exists. In fact, there are people who choose to convert to Christianity once they enter a college science program or medical school. A naturalistic world view just does not add up to the scientific evidence. Only the existence of God gives an adequate explanation for how the world works. Christians need to stop fighting science and learn to embrace it instead.

By rebelling against science, Christians are rebelling against the gifts God bestowed on them. God created human beings in His image. Therefore, human beings possess the ability to think, explore, and understand to a depth that no other animal is capable. Science allows humans to use God's gifts in order to think, explore, and understand the world God created. But God didn't just create the Earth and the creatures on it. God created the entire universe. Another reason for the Christian fear of science is that we might not be alone in the universe.

Since the advent of space exploration in the twentieth century, the possibility of human beings coming into contact with extraterrestrials has filled the human imagination. The odds seem to indicate that with the sheer number of galaxies, stars, and planets in existence there should be more than just human beings capable of space travel. If there are other creatures out there, then how do they relate to God? Did God create them? Do they believe in God? If these extraterrestrials make contact, will it mean that God doesn't exist? Is God an extraterrestrial? These questions might scare some Christians, but they need not worry. Nothing will change regarding God even if extraterrestrials make contact.

God existed before anything else. This is an important tenet of Christianity. So if you believe that God existed before anything else then that means that God created the universe and whoever inhabits other planets. It makes sense that if there are going to be a great deal of galaxies then God would choose to populate planets with creatures. Otherwise it would just be a great deal of meaningless empty space. What about the relationship between humans and God if humans suddenly discover there are creatures living on other planets?

The relationship does not change. God made a covenant with Adam and Eve. He made a covenant with Abraham. He made a covenant with King David. He made a covenant with gentiles, sealed with the blood of Jesus Christ. None of this changes. God has always lived up to His end of the bargain. It has been humanity that has failed in keeping up its end. The Bible is the story of God's relationship with His people. Therefore nothing about extraterrestrials, dinosaurs, or other ancient civilizations is included. Nothing will change between God and His people if suddenly extraterrestrials show up on Earth. God created these extraterrestrials. They either worship God or reject Him or they have some other relationship with Him. Perhaps all of this is just speculation and God has divided the galaxies in such a way that His creations on separate planets will never communicate with one another. In all likelihood, you will never see an extraterrestrial in your lifetime. So if this is a major issue in your conversion to Christianity then my suggestion is that you focus on what you can control, the way you choose to live your Earthly life, and stop worrying about what you can't control, the existence of extraterrestrials.

Similarly, other scientific "what if" discoveries will not change the covenant God made between Himself and humanity. The two largest fears are probably what if science proves that there is no afterlife, therefore no heaven and hell, or what if science even proves there is no God. Again, there is no use to worry or give these "what ifs" a lot of thought. They simply will never come true in your lifetime – if ever.

Perhaps the greatest fear Christians have about science is that it will one day prove that God does not exist. This will never happen. The evidence is too strong for the existence of God. The evidence is too strong for the existence of Jesus of Nazareth. As long as there is a historical Jesus, then there will always be those who believe in his being the Son of God. There cannot be a Son of God if there is no God. Fearing science for what it might discover is wrong because of the great good that it can tell us about God's world. In the future, science will do more to drive people to Christianity and prove the existence of God than it will disprove the existence of God.

12 A PRESCRIPTION FOR CHRISTIANS

Throughout this book I have tackled questions of belief. Those concepts that you should believe in, such as creationism, the historical Jesus, the Bible as eyewitness testimony, suffering, heaven and hell, and angels and demons. One of the most difficult parts of being a Christian is believing day-in and day-out. It can be fairly easy to believe initially. Maybe you have a "come to Jesus moment." You or a family member becomes extremely sick, but suddenly makes a recovery. During the process of this recovery you are able to see God at work. Or maybe you are like me and needed to read through the scholarship about the historical Jesus. After reading the arguments for and against the existence of Jesus of Nazareth, I came to the conclusion that Jesus was real and his teachings were sound. Therefore, God existed and I had to believe in Him. Perhaps you are like Moses and need God to speak your language through a burning bush. Whichever way it happens, God will reach out and speak to you. It is up to you to heed the call and come to Him. But what happens once you come to Him? It can be a lot of work to continually believe in God in the twenty-first century. This chapter will give you some tips on how to keep your beliefs in a world that is becoming increasingly hostile toward Christianity.

Now the main culprit hindering belief in God is the twenty-four hour news media. I am not blaming any single news outlet or personality. These people are just doing their jobs. The Internet and cable news channels need content to fill twenty-four hours each day. The surest way to fill that time is to find a controversial story in which one side can be pitted against another. It might not involve a modicum of truth, but it will be interesting and is sure to spark debate. Debates can turn an insignificant story into a bigger story. This bigger story can take up multiple hours of a day or even run for several days until a new story takes its place. In the grand scheme of things, these small stories that grow bigger and bigger are not all that important. It is our reaction to them that inflates their importance.

For example, an atheist or atheist organization hires a lawyer to sue the government for having a statue of the Ten Commandments outside a government building. This is always good for a story. A news outlet has a ready-made debate. There are the atheists who are bringing the lawsuit in the name of separation of church and state. Then there are the Christians who claim that the laws of the United States are based upon the Ten Commandments. One side finds the statue outside a government building to be offensive, the other a necessary reminder of where our laws come from. This debate can role on for several hours, days, weeks, or even months while the court reaches a decision. The news media eats this up. They have a story to fill their time slots. Unfortunately, there are too many people who are drawn into stories like this. Those who get involved in debates like this need to take a step back. If a statue of the Ten Commandments is left in front of a government building or taken down it will have no bearing on your personal beliefs. God will still exist even if the statue of the Ten Commandments is taken down.

God is God and He is not going anywhere. He called you to come home and you heeded the call. You will struggle at times in your life to believe in the truth of God, but that does not mean that He doesn't exist or that He doesn't continue to love you. Like those who get caught up in the twenty-four hour news stories that have little meaning, the problem is with you and not the media or God. You are the one who needs to change your attitude.

Reading is the surest way for me to strengthen my belief in God. Whenever I have a doubt, I turn to a book to guide me. Besides the Bible, I typically look for some work written by an apologetic. Apologetics is the defense of the Christian faith. It comes from the Greek word for defense. I am partial to the works of C.S. Lewis. Lewis was an atheist, but converted to Christianity later in life. He taught literature at Cambridge. Being a former atheist, and someone with a good deal of intelligence, it is comforting to read Lewis' arguments for the existence of God. *Mere Christianity* is his masterwork when it comes to Christian apologetics, but just about any book or essay he wrote on the subject is worth reading. He presents his arguments in an easy to follow, logical way that is often missing when reading other works on God — especially those written by atheists.

Reading the writings of atheists can also strengthen your faith. I have read many works by atheists who attempt to disprove the historicity of Jesus of Nazareth. Many of the theories that I have read are comical. They postulate that if this happened or if this other thing happened then perhaps you can come to a conclusion that Jesus of Nazareth never existed. Some of these books include *The Jesus Puzzle* and *The Jesus Question*. These far-fetched books are great in strengthening your belief as you can see how atheists have to mangle historical facts in order to fit their ideas.

Certainly the most important book that all Christians must read frequently is the Bible. Sitting in church each week and listening to a Biblical story is not enough. You have to be proactive in your faith. God will come to you and speak your language, but you have to come to Him to continually believe and get the most out of your earthly relationship with Him. You can read the Bible over continuously throughout your life and still learn something new each time you read. This is because the Bible will speak to you in different ways depending on what you are going through in your life. The reason why the Bible has lasted for so many years, and is so powerful, is because of the universality of its message.

Personally, I prefer reading the Gospels. These four books are the most important of the Christian faith. Although some intelligent and pious people wrote the other books of the Bible, the Gospels are the only direct accounts of the life of the Son of God. As such, I place their teachings above anything else in the Bible. Now you do not have to do as I have, but you do need to understand how important the Gospels are to Christianity. I started reading the Bible from the beginning at Genesis, but quickly became tired of the rules and census writings of Leviticus and Numbers. I flipped forward to the New Testament and read the four Gospels. From there, everything else seemed to fit into place. Even a book as difficult as Revelations was easy to read after finishing the Gospels. If I had started with Revelations or tried to push through with the rest of the Old Testament, then I can tell you that I probably would not be a Christian right now. A book like Revelations is too radical for my belief and reasoning. It seems like a work of fiction. The Gospels do not have the tenets of a fictional story. They come from eyewitness testimony and because of this they are easier to believe. The fact that they are telling the story of the Son of God makes them even more powerful.

Now, I prefer the New Testament to the Old Testament. The four Gospels and the letters written by Paul and other early church leaders are interesting and filled with practical advice that can be readily applied to my own life. The same is not true of the Old Testament. As a historian I can appreciate the historical stories of the Bible. Exodus with the stories of Moses leading the Israelites out of Egypt is great. I also enjoy reading about King David and King Solomon. It is the non-historical books that I struggle with. Books like Proverbs and Psalms are interesting and full of practical advice, so they're alright. It's the books filled with teachings from the prophets that I struggle with. A great deal of these books were written at a time when the Israelites were away from the Holy Land. They were dealing with God's wrath and trying to make sense of their fate. Like all of the Bible, these books are necessary to read, but they can be difficult. They are the books that I need someone with a degree in divinity studies to tell me why they are so important. There is one exception though. The Book of

Job is perhaps the best book of the Old Testament. It is not a book written by a prophet, nor does it really fit into the historical story of the Israelites. However, I am sure that it is the most potent book in the Old Testament for those who struggle with belief.

The Book of Job opens with a conversation between God and the Satan. Satan complains that it is easy for someone to believe in God when God gives this person everything they desire. God says this is not true. As a test, God tells Satan to do whatever he wishes to Job, just so long as he isn't killed. For the majority of his life, Job has been a pious and prosperous man. He is rich. He has a large farm. He has a beautiful family. Then Satan gets involved. The fortune is lost. The farm finds drought. The family is killed. Job is made sick and forced to bed rest for several months. He emerges from bed covered with ugly boils. A few of his friends stop by to find him in this bad state. They point out that God is not good and that it is because of God that Job has suffered so much. Job wants to agree with them, but he cannot believe that God would punish an innocent person. Although Job's friends have no problems cursing God, Job will not resort to that type of self-pity. Then God speaks to Job and his companions. Job's friends are cursed for having little faith. God tells Job what happened to him. Job does not like this explanation. But God is God. Job is not God. You are not God. So it does not matter if Job or you or me object to the way God works. God is God and God will not change just because you have a disagreement with how He made the world work. Although Job does not appreciate the way he has been treated, he is willing to accept that this is God's world and it is his responsibility to live in that world. This is a powerful message for those struggling to sustain belief in God.

The Book of Job teaches us that this is God's world and that we must submit to God. There is no use fighting or wishing for other options. Often we struggle with the idea that this is God's world. We cannot see God. We cannot have a two-way conversation with God in the same way we can with other human beings. We live in a world full of technology and twenty-four hour news cycles. It is difficult to remain faithful to God. Yet we must. We must because it is God's world. By reading the Book of Job we are able to clearly get this message. God asks Job if he can control the winds or if he can create the stars. Job replies that he cannot. God says that He can because He is God. The argument is over. So if the Gospels don't help strengthen your belief, flip over to the Book of Job in the Old Testament and you will emerge a stronger Christian.

Another way to become a stronger Christian is to attend church each Sunday. This can be difficult. It seems like each month there is a new scandal hitting the church. A priest is exposed as an adulterer or a priest says something that manages to anger a great deal of the population. There is also the issue of having to give up a Sunday morning to go to church.

Your time is scarce and you might not make church a priority when there is so much to do at home or work on the weekend. Then there is the issue of finding a church. You have to find one that features a pastor who speaks about God in a way that you can relate. You also have to find one that has all the features you want. Maybe you need one with a daycare for the children, or a strong Sunday school program. Perhaps Bible study groups are more your thing. Maybe you want a small church or you love crowds and want to be part of one of the mega churches. Whatever your wants, finding a church can be a long and difficult process. Just remember that if you put in the effort then you will be rewarded.

The reward might not come immediately though. You will have to continually work to find what you need. I remember the first time I stepped into church I felt intimidated. I had worked with one of the pastors previously. I had played on the church's softball team, so I knew some of the parishioners. But it was still church. I was nervous. My first words to the head pastor were: "Eric said it was alright for me to be here." I asked for permission to come to church. I knew no better though. Despite my resistance and feelings of intimidation, I persisted and forced myself to get out of bed each Sunday and make the drive to church. Going to church paid off. It wasn't an immediate or material pay-off. Instead, it was a change of attitude.

I used to get frustrated while driving in traffic. My road rage was not severe enough where I would pull over and accost another driver. Instead, I filled my car with profanity and my heart with hate. After going to church for a few months I found my road rage greatly diminished. I was no longer frustrated by the driving habits of those I couldn't control. I was no longer anxious about getting to my destination on time. I wouldn't allow the little annoyances of other drivers get under my skin. Going to church taught me patience. Each week I heard about the impatience and frailties of human beings and how patient God was with them. If God could be patient with a whole group of people who He loved, then I could be patient with drivers I'd never met and probably would never interact with again.

Getting involved with a connect group also helped develop my faith in God. It was one thing to listen to the pastor's sermon each Sunday. It was another to try and live up to the words of the sermon and the teachings of Jesus. Being around a small group of people who were there to help one another in their belief in God was just what I needed to keep me on the Christian path. My connect group was composed of about ten other people who attended the church. Since I was single, I was put into the group typically reserved for single people. Despite that, the group was diverse. There were older people than me. There were younger people than me. There were a few couples. Some had kids. Really all that tied us together was our being Christian. The group met each Sunday after the service. We would spend some time talking about each of our weeks and then discuss what we thought about the sermon and how it might impact our lives in the coming week. The group would also meet at someone's home each week for a Bible study.

As someone who was struggling at times to believe and who had plenty of doubts, this group really helped break down my resistance. The diversity of the group and the closeness of the group were what helped swing me toward believing in God. I was around more mature Christians. Many in the group had been believers for their entire lives. Some came to Christianity later in life and knew what I was going through. Talking about my doubts really helped develop my faith. I found out that they had their own doubts. Even those who had been Christians for a long time still had doubts. But at the end of the day, these doubts didn't matter compared to what they knew about God. They knew that God existed. They knew that God was love. They knew that as much as they wished, they could not control the world – only God can.

Being part of a connect group was also liberating. The group was composed of people who were just like me. There were no church authority figures in the group. The pastor would come to the discussions after the sermon sometimes, but he was not a pillar of the group. Being able to discuss our beliefs without having a traditional church authority present was liberating because we could be honest. Sometimes there is a feeling that we have to walk on eggshells around a pastor out of fear that we might offend him or he might cast judgment on us for something we say. So by not having a pastor present, the connect group fostered a feeling of safety. When we gathered at a person's house for Bible study there was always food and wine for those who wished to socialize while reading God's word. I definitely recommend you try a connect group or Bible study group in addition to going to church. It's a great way to socialize with other Christians, develop your understanding of the Bible, and strengthen your belief.

It is great to read about the historical Jesus, read the Bible, attend church, and connect with other Christians. But all of this is meaningless unless you act like a Christian. All the research and talk of Christianity pales in comparison to living the teachings of Christ. St. Francis of Assisi is attributed with the saying: "Preach the Gospel, and if necessary, use words." Immersing yourself in a Christian lifestyle is the surest way to strengthening your belief and getting the most out of life.

So how do you live the Christian life? The Bible and church attendance can be guides, but Jesus synthesized it all into the phrase: "Love God and love others." This seems easy, but is hard. You will feel betrayed by God and other people. You will wake up hating what someone has done to you. Despite this, you have to love God and the people who hurt you.

You have to constantly work to keep Jesus' maxim. It isn't easy to be a Christian. It is difficult to believe, but even more difficult to keep believing and living like a Christian. You have to remain committed to Christ so that you do not fall.

Immersing yourself in a Christian lifestyle and God is the surest way to remain on track. This means talking with, but also observing, other Christians. How do other Christians treat their fellow human beings? You do not judge them – just observe. If they treat their fellow humans with respect and love, then try to mimic them.

You can also immerse yourself in the word of God through constant reading of the Bible, books on Christian living, and discussions with your pastor. Your pastor is there to provide you with advice on how to live a Christian lifestyle. He doesn't just work one hour a week. He should be there for you when you have a problem, or when you just want to talk. Do not forget about your pastor and how important he can be in your growth as a Christian.

Another tough part about trying to live a Christian life is keeping focused on the big picture. This is a world that is built on the short-term. We live in a technologically advanced society in which news and opinions are only as far away as a mouse click on Facebook or Twitter. The capitalist system is built on short-term gratification. If your company is able to meet its numbers in the first quarter then there is a chance that you will be promoted. If your company doesn't meet its numbers in the first quarter, then you could be out of a job. It is difficult to think of the long-term when short-term ideals are so prized in this world. It is this long-term view that makes Christianity worth pursuing.

If you have come this far then I hope that you are seriously considering becoming a Christian. Here are three ideas that you can take away with you as you continue to do research into Christianity. First, just because God is not physically visible does not mean that He is not real. Think of the Israelites who saw the miracle of the parting of the Red Sea, yet still doubted in God. Or think of Jesus' disciples who weren't completely sure about him until he died. Seeing is not always believing, especially when it comes to God. Second, remember that this is God's world and not yours. Think of Job. God told Job that He created the world. He asked Job if Job could create the world. Job couldn't and neither can you. Only God can. Remember that and so much of the pressure of everyday life will be taken off your shoulders. Lastly, remember the big picture and not the small picture. This is a further way in which you can give up control. Once you understand these three concepts, you can focus on them as you progress in life. You will live a more fulfilling and pleasant life through following God.

ABOUT THE AUTHOR

Steven M. Painter converted to Christianity in 2013. He has a bachelor's degree in journalism from the University of New Mexico and a master's degree in media arts from the University of Arizona. He has worked as a journalist, book editor, and is currently a high school social studies teacher in Tucson, Arizona.

He has published two previous works. Take Her For a Ride is a novel set in 1930s Hollywood and was published in 2013. Its sequel, Blonde Ash, was published in 2014.

When not teaching or writing, Painter enjoys watching and playing sports (especially basketball), watching classic movies, and hiking around the deserts of the southwest.

For more information, check out his website at www.stevenmpainter.com.

www.ingramcontent.com/pod-product-compliance
Lightning Source LLC
Chambersburg PA
CBHW060332050426
42449CB00011B/2738